THE

Strenuous Life

HANDBOOK

BADGES

THE
STRENUOUS LIFE
CREED

I live The Strenuous Life.
I train for harmony in body, mind, and soul.
I am strong to be useful.
I choose action over abstraction.
I do hard things.

I LIVE THE STRENUOUS LIFE.

WELCOME TO THE
STRENUOUS LIFE

The Strenuous Life is the antidote to the feelings of malaise that pervade our modern society.

It's a protest against a culture that pushes passivity, comfort, and retreat into abstraction at the detriment of our mental, physical, and spiritual well-being.

The Strenuous Life is a resistance movement that aims to reconnect individuals to the beating heart of reality. It demands that men get outside of their heads in order to experience the tangible world on its most vivid and intense terms.

The Strenuous Life demands that followers do hard things. It's a structured program designed to push individuals beyond their comfort zone and develop every aspect of who they are. Adherents are expected to train their bodies with vigorous exercise, train their minds and muscles by learning new skills, and train their souls by living a life of service-seeking virtue.

The Strenuous Life pushes back against the prevailing paradigm of modern life that encourages self-absorbed ease. Instead of a frictionless digital utopia in which every one of our desires can be fulfilled with a click of a mouse, The Strenuous Life seeks out challenge in the concrete world. For it is only through rubbing up against things that make us physically and mentally uncomfortable that we become sharper and keener.

I promise as you seek to live The Strenuous Life, you'll find yourself feeling more empowered, confident, and effective in your world. The change won't happen right away, but it will come. The Strenuous Life won't always be easy, but it will certainly be worth it.

Best of luck on your journey in living The Strenuous Life!

Yours in Strenuosity,
Brett H. McKay
Chief Guide, The Strenuous Life

HOW TO FOLLOW THE STRENUOUS LIFE PROGRAM

The Strenuous Life takes a balanced, three-pronged approach in forging strong and well-rounded men. This consists of a "whole man"-focused training program that centers on physical culture, skill development, and moral discipline.

ENTERING THE GYMNASIUM

The Strenuous Life forum is called the Gymnasium. In ancient Greece, gymnasia constituted *the* meeting place for men. Here athletes, warriors, artists, and philosophers all rubbed shoulders, for the gymnasium was a place not only for athletic training, but education as well, and often combined schools of philosophy with run-

Note: Instructions in this handbook are aimed toward members of The Strenuous Life online forum, or Gymnasium. You are more than welcome to use this handbook for offline clubs and affiliations, and for personal use. Simply modify the requirements to fit your individual needs. However, only members of the Gymnasium are eligible to receive physical badges for the completion of each badge's requirements.

ning tracks and wrestling grounds. The nature of these meeting places was based on the Greek motto of *"Mens sana in corpore sano"* or "A strong mind in a strong body." Their ideal of manhood was to harmonize one's physical, mental, and moral qualities—to circumscribe all excellences into a balanced whole.

Over the entrance to one private and elite gymnasium was inscribed this injunction: "Strip or retire." The ancient Grecians used to compete in sports and exercise in the nude, and in fact the word gymnasium is derived from the Greek for "to train naked." Thus, the inscription served as a challenge to each man entering this exclusive arena: come in, participate, and struggle—or keep out. Mere spectators were not welcome.

To be part of the gymnasium, you were literally required to put your skin in the game.

The Strenuous Life Gymnasium upholds these same ideals. Members are encouraged towards well-rounded development, and are charged with putting their skin in the game. It isn't a place for passive onlookers. It's a gathering for those who are truly committed to challenging themselves and growing in all aspects of their lives.

Physical Culture

Physical fitness plays an integral role in The Strenuous Life. Development of the body serves as a foundation for the development of one's mental and spiritual capacities.

In our modern world, it's possible to go through everyday life without exerting yourself at all. You roll out of bed to sit in the seat of your car, which takes you to your seat at work, and then you come home to your seat on the sofa. As you slide through this sedentary, frictionless existence, life starts to feel unreal, tiresome, and unsatisfying. It's hard not to even feel an element of self-disgust at the meager tasks your body—an anatomical wonder capable of lifting, running, crawling, jumping, fighting, throwing, swimming, and more—has been consigned to. It's no wonder that a lack of physical activity has been linked with depression and anxiety.

Exercise kills these mental maladies and reawakens your physical potential. It reconnects you with your body and the tangible universe. When you feel your blood pumping and heart pounding, when you feel the sweat dripping off your forehead, you come back to yourself. In a world that lacks innate challenges, exercise furnishes a needed set; you once again get to test yourself as you strive to lift the weight, clear the hurdle, beat the clock.

What's more, the discipline that you develop while sticking to a regular fitness program will carry over to other domains. As you exercise consistently, you'll find yourself becoming more consistent in your work and family life. As you push your body harder than you thought possible, you'll find yourself being able to break through plateaus in other areas of your life too. The confidence that you gain through regular physical training will make you more confident overall.

As adherents of The Strenuous Life, we work out not merely to attain aesthetic effects (though this can be a wonderful byproduct), or because it feels good (though it definitely does), or even because it's crucial for good health (which it assuredly is). We exercise our bodies to enhance our ability to think clearly, to master temptations and weaknesses, and to serve others. We become strong, as 19th century physical culturist Georges Hebert put it, to be useful. This is true functional fitness. This is training with a higher purpose.

Living The Strenuous Life requires committing yourself to one hour of physical activity each day.

Each day when you sign-in to strenuouslife.co, you will be required to check in as to whether or not you've done your one hour of physical training. The number of times you successfully complete 60 minutes of physical activity a day will be recorded and reflected on your Class leaderboard. Your answer to this check-in question is based completely on the honor system. Don't act with shame and cheat yourself by lying to this question.

The sort of physical activity you do is up to you. Weightlifting, CrossFit, running, kettlebells, boxing, hiking, swimming, a vigorous walk—even roughhousing with your kids. They all count. Just put in an hour each day.

With that said, we do strongly recommend that you incorporate some sort of strength training in your exercise routine. Strength is the foundation of all other fitness modalities. And as *Starting Strength* author Mark Rippetoe has noted, "strong people are harder to kill than weak people and more useful in general."

We also recommend that you find ways to do your physical training outside as much as you can. Nothing reconnects the mind and body to primal reality like exercising in the wild. While you might not be able to do your barbell program outside, make sure to find ways to move more in nature. Do one of your weekly runs on a trail. Or spend your recovery day taking an hour-long hike in a nearby nature preserve. Test yourself in different environments and with different elements. Walk barefoot in the woods. Run in the rain. Do a pull-up on a tree branch. Balance on a log. Take a swim in a cold pond.

Skill Development

> *"Skilled practices serve as an anchor to the world beyond one's head—a point of triangulation with objects and other people who have a reality of their own."*
>
> —*Matthew B. Crawford*

The Strenuous Life aims to increase the agency and autonomy of its followers. We want to see individuals who have the competency and confidence to actively shape the world as they envision instead of passively letting the world shape them. We want to fight back against the tide that has moved us further away from the beating heart of things. We want men who are active participants in life and not mere spectators.

Part of the malaise that many men feel in today's modern world is that they simply don't have any control over their lives. They struggle to be self-starters and don't believe they can make things happen for themselves. There's a feeling that some anonymous person or organization is pulling all the levers on their lives, and that problems can only be fixed by appealing to third parties for help. They feel impotent and helpless.

The antidote to these feelings of powerlessness is to increase the amount of skills at our disposal. Nietzsche once said that "happiness is the feeling of power increasing." As we increase the amount of skills we have, we increase our power to have an effect on the world. And that potency feels good. Really good.

Living The Strenuous Life requires dedicating yourself to constant skill acquisition and practice.

To help followers of The Strenuous Life become more skillful and self-directed, we've created 50+ badges covering skills we believe will help men live a more fulfilled life, stay ever ready for any scenario, and be of greater service to others. You'll find the requirements for each badge in the pages that follow and at strenuouslife.co.

Completion of the requirements is based on the honor system. Only you can judge whether you've done the necessary work for a requirement. Err on the side of doing too much, rather than doing too little.

In general, all requirements must be completed *after* you've started the badge. Even if you've already done 30 hours of community service in your life, you'll have to do another 30 to earn the Community Service Badge.

With that said, some requirements are of the "one and done" variety (e.g. getting a motorcycle license, building a chicken coop, starting a business, etc.). For those types of requirements, if you've already done them, feel free to mark them as entirely complete, or complete the part of the requirement you haven't done and/or that you can still do (e.g., even if you've already built a chicken coop, you still have to harvest the eggs; even if you've already started a business, you still have to get to the point where you're making $1,000 a month on it.)

If you're not sure whether one or more of a badge's requirements that you've already done prior to beginning the badge must be competed again, use your best judgement and follow your conscience. When in doubt, we again strongly suggest erring on the side of doing too much, rather than doing too little, and doing the requirement again, especially if it's been a while since you did it. This is The Strenuous Life after all! Skills and knowledge degrade over the years, so revisiting them acts as an important refresher. Finally, if you've already done most of a badge's requirements, consider choosing another badge in order to give yourself a greater challenge.

To repeat the overarching principle of TSL: Don't act shamefully by lying; you're not only cheating your fellow comrades in The Strenuous Life, you're cheating yourself out of attaining true competence in a skill and enjoying the satisfaction of unfettered achievement.

Each badge will require that you submit at least one piece of photographic evidence to the Gymnasium showing your work on the badge's requirements. (There are a couple badges that require a short written essay in lieu of this photograph.) It could be a picture of a completed project or a picture of you in the process of doing one of the requirements. Feel free to upload more photos to show your fellow comrades what you've been working on. The rest of the requirements are based purely on the honor system.

While completion of a Strenuous Life Badge will get you competent in that area, it won't necessarily mean you've completely mastered that particular skill. These badges are designed to offer participants an introduction to different domains. We encourage individuals to continue to explore and push themselves in that area even after they've earned a badge.

Once you've completed all the requirements for a badge, you can purchase an actual physical badge, so, so that you can have a tangible reminder of your skill development and achievement.

Moral Discipline

> *"But, in the long run, in the great battle of life, no brilliancy of intellect, no perfection of bodily development, will count when weighed in the balance against that assemblage of virtues, active and passive, of moral qualities, which we group together under the name of character."*
>
> —*Theodore Roosevelt*

Not only do we want to help shape men who are strong in body and mind, we also want to help build men who are strong in character. The Strenuous Life is a revolt against the self-indulgent morality that only looks out for oneself. We exhort men to have noble and good aims and to daily strive after them, even when it's inconvenient. Virtue, duty, and service over self-gratification.

Selfless self-improvement is our mantra, and rather than constituting a contradiction, these aims actually go hand-in-hand; while service and self-improvement are so often disconnected in the modern world, the former forms the brightest and surest path to the latter. As we seek to become more fit, skilled, temperate, frugal, patient, courageous, resolute, and honest, we strengthen and improve our families, communities, and country. At the same time, we move closer to what the Greeks called *eudaimonia*, or human flourishing—and we experience the fulfillment and sense of worth attendant to that state. As Theodore Roosevelt, the patron saint of The Strenuous Life noted: "Happiness and usefulness are largely found in the same soul."

Living The Strenuous Life requires forging your moral discipline and seeking to do a good deed every day.

At the beginning of each day ask yourself the question Benjamin Franklin contemplated each morning: "What good shall I do this day?" Your act of service doesn't have to be big (though bully for you stepping in to handle something that is!). It could be as simple as writing a note of encouragement to a co-worker who you know is having a rough go right now, picking up someone's dropped items, or surprising your significant other with a home cooked meal. At the end of each day, you should be able to recount at least one way you put yourself to use, and when you sign in to strenuouslife.co, you will be asked whether or not you have. The number of times you successfully do a daily good deed will be recorded and reflected on your Class leaderboard. Your answer to this check-in question is based on honor, and on this, of all things, you should answer with integrity.

The Agon

TSL's fitness requirement, badges, and daily good deed challenge will all motivate you to develop yourself in body, mind, and spirit. But there's one more element designed to bolster your training and development: the Agon.

In ancient Greece, the agon was a struggle or contest that would test a man's bodily or mental toughness and prowess in athletics, art, music, debate, and more.

In The Strenuous Life, the Agon is a weekly challenge that will push you outside your comfort zone mentally or physically. At the end of each week, you'll be sent a link where you can view that week's Agon. Should you accept and complete this mission, you can mark it off on the TSL platform, and the number of Agons you've successfully completed will be reported on your Class leaderboard.

Your Class Leaderboard

> "Life is a game with a glorious prize,
> If we can only play it right.
> It is give and take, build and break,
> And often it ends in a fight;
> But he surely wins who honestly tries
> (Regardless of wealth or fame),
> He can never despair who plays it fair
> How are you playing the game?"
> —Anonymous, c. 1900

At the turn of the 20th century, adherents of strenuosity often referred to life as a game. You faced hard knocks, competed against foes, gave your all, and remained a good sportsman even when you fell short. Most of all, you

---

played in the arena with vim, vigor, and energy, relished the struggle, and had a heck of a lot of fun along the way.

We've built The Strenuous Life program around the same principles. It's a challenge and a test and a competition, and it should push you outside your comfort zone. But it's also designed to be a game. One you'll have a good time playing.

In your Class, you'll find a leaderboard that displays how many daily fitness and good deed check-ins you've done, how many badges you've earned, and how many weekly Agons you've completed

The goal of the leaderboard is two-fold. First, it's a concrete metric that helps keep you accountable and allows you to see your progress in living The Strenuous Life. The higher a participant's numbers are, the more he's been pushing himself and taking action. "Gamifying" tasks has been proven to keep people more motivated in sticking with them.

Second, the leaderboard injects a bit of healthy competition amongst Class members. When you see that another man is climbing up the leaderboard due to his consistent action, it'll spur you to live more strenuously yourself.

Is there a prize for being at the top of the leaderboard? Maybe. But it will be a surprise if it happens. This isn't Chuck E. Cheese's. You're a grown man. Besting your fellows, and most importantly, becoming a better man, should be reward enough.

Support and Edify Your Class

> *"For the strength of the pack is the wolf, and the strength of the wolf is the pack."*
>
> —*Rudyard Kipling*

When you register with The Strenuous Life, you'll be assigned to a Class. This will be your digital company while you're with us at TSL. Your classmates will be your competitors and comrades.

Each Class will cap at 150 members. We want to keep these groups relatively small to ensure that guys can get to know each other and that no one gets lost in the digital ether.

Each Class will have their own forum where comrades can interact with each other. Your Class is where you can share what you're working on in The Strenuous Life and ask for advice on things you're struggling with. Treat your class like a "mastermind" by sharing your big picture goals and asking your compatriots to hold you accountable to them.

Besides taking from the collective pot by asking for advice, be sure to put something back in by providing encouragement, support, and edification to your fellow classmates. Celebrate victories. Offer constructive feedback when it's asked for. Provide a hand of fellowship when a comrade experiences a setback. Offer supportive accountability when guys start slipping off track. Live by the Latin maxim, *si vales, valeo*. When you are strong, I am strong.

In all of your interactions with your classmates, maintain civility and respect. A little good-natured razzing and tough love talk is fine and a healthy part of manly camaraderie, but don't let it digress into juvenile sniping and trolling. If it does, you will be given a warning. After that, you'll be expelled from The Strenuous Life.

In addition to being your fellow travelers in The Strenuous Life, your classmates will also be your competitors. "Each Class will have a leaderboard that indicates the number of badges, Agons, and physical and good-deed check-ins each classmate has completed. Compete for bragging rights on who is living most strenuously.

While digital interactions are no substitute for face-to-face ones, it's better than nothing. We highly encourage you to meet up with your fellow classmates in person if and when possible.

The Honor System

Everything in The Strenuous Life operates on the honor system. When it comes to checking in for your daily physical activity and good deed, the achievement of the Agon, and the earning of badges, you're on your honor when swearing to whether you did these things or not. If you lie, fudge, or hedge in a way you know deep down is wrong, you cheat your fellow classmates, and you cheat yourself. You climb the leaderboard while cankering your soul.

If you can't complete a badge requirement exactly how it's laid out, it's entirely up to your conscience as to whether a modified or alternative substitute should still be counted. Do your best to fulfill the requirement both by the letter and by the spirit, and make exceptions only when absolutely, positively necessary. If you're not sure, ask your classmates what they think. We trust that you'll let your sense of honor guide you on whether you've done enough to complete a requirement or not.

If you believe one of your classmates has been cheating in the earning of their badges/Agons/check-ins, you should first confront them yourself about your concerns. Issues of honor are resolved man-to-man, not by running to a third party to mediate the dispute. Appeal to your classmates for help, and work out the problem within your Class. If, after absolutely exhausting all possibilities to resolve the issue within your Class, the problem remains, you may then, and only then, contact an administrator to step in.

Keep your honor strenuously.

THE BADGES

ANCESTRY BADGE

Up until the 20th century, a man's roots—his ancestry—formed an important part of his identity. Noble families in ancient Rome displayed wax masks of their ancestors in their homes as reminders of their legacy. In ancient Japan, ancestor worship was common and families fiercely guarded the scrolls that contained their genealogy. The goal in life was to live in a way that would bring honor to the family.

In the 19th century, it was common for homes in Europe and the U.S. to prominently display a family Bible that had been passed down through the generations with names of deceased ancestors inscribed in the front. Parents and grandparents told children and grandchildren stories about the brave deeds done by their ancestors and the dignified lives previous generations had lived, admonishing them to never act in a way that would sully their lineage.

In the hyper-individualistic and present-focused culture of the 21st century, interest in one's heritage and family ties has waned—to our detriment. Research suggests that when we have an intimate knowledge of our family history, we feel more self-confident compared to individuals who don't. There's something about understanding your past and knowing you belong to a story bigger than yourself that instills confidence and motivates you to be your best.

The Ancestry Badge will put you on the path of honoring your ancestors, creating a fuller, richer, and timeless identity for yourself, and leaving a legacy to those who will come after you.

ANCESTRY BADGE REQUIREMENTS

Complete 9 of the following requirements:

1. Visit your local library (many have a genealogical division) or a genealogy website to start researching your family tree.
2. Fill out family group sheets on both sides of your family going back at least 3 generations.
3. Complete your family tree on both your father and mother's side going back at least 3 generations.
4. Obtain copies of at least 2 important genealogical records from 2 of your ancestors. (Birth certificate, marriage certificate, immigration certificate, etc.)
5. Begin a family history photo collection by obtaining at least 5 photos of your ancestors, from at least your grandparents generation and older. You are also encouraged, though not required, to hang some of these photos up in your home.
6. Interview 2 older relatives about your family's history. Audio or video record the conversations.
7. Obtain a family heirloom, learn the story behind it, and display it in a place where you can see it regularly.
8. Find out the meaning and history of your surname on both your father's and mother's side. If your family has

a crest, badge, or motto, research its meaning. You are also encouraged, but not required, to display it somewhere in your home.

9. Reach out to a confirmed distant relative. Exchange genealogical information.

10. Complete the Journaling Badge to start a record of your life for your posterity.

11. Get your genome sequenced to discover your genetic genealogy.

For additional resources, visit stren.life/ancestry.

ANGLER BADGE

Whether he likes to dip his pole into ocean, lake, or stream, fishing can play a wonderful role in a man's life. It offers a relaxing hobby, a chance to spend time in the great outdoors, the opportunity to re-connect with his primal hunting side (hunting includes nabbing the creatures of both land *and* water!), and even food for his table.

ANGLER BADGE REQUIREMENTS

Complete all of the following requirements:

1. Catch and identify 3 different species of fish, caught using at least 2 different legal, sportsman-like methods (fly-casting, bait-casting, trolling, net fishing, etc.). At least one of the fish must be taken by fly or bait-casting.
2. Make at least 1 artificial bait lure and catch a fish with it (can count towards the 3 above).
3. Catch and identify at least 3 kinds of live bait.
4. Clean, cook, and eat at least 1 fish you caught.

For additional resources, visit stren.life/angler.

ARCHERY BADGE

For thousands of years, humans have used the bow and arrow for hunting and warfare. While modern firearms certainly pack more punch, there's still a good case to be made for a man being proficient in the art of archery. Like a firearm, a bow and arrow can be used for acquiring food or even for self-defense, but it also offers unique benefits as well.

For starters, it's silent. When you're hunting, keeping a low profile with a bow and arrow will ensure that you don't scare away your prey.

With a bow and arrow, you can re-use your arrows after you shoot them. This could come in handy when you're in the wild for extended periods of time. With a firearm, once your bullets are gone, they're gone until you can buy some more.

There's also a lot less legal red tape with a bow and arrow than with a firearm. You don't need to undergo a background check to buy a bow nor do you need a special permit to carry one around (if for some reason you decided to walk around town with a bow).

Finally, there's something about shooting a bow that's just plain enjoyable. Yes, shooting firearms is incredibly fun, but the quietness of drawing back your bow and letting an arrow fly lends itself to a more relaxed, almost meditative experience.

With the Archery Badge, you'll learn everything you need to know to use a bow and arrow for fun, sport, survival, or achieving zen-like flow.

ARCHERY BADGE REQUIREMENTS

Complete all of the following requirements:

1. Name the parts of a traditional recurve bow or compound bow.
2. Name the parts of an arrow.
3. Explain the basics of archery safety to a friend.
4. Determine your draw length.
5. Demonstrate the proper way to string a recurve or longbow.
6. Using a 300 Round target at a distance of 20 yards and with only 30 arrows attain the minimum scores using one of the following bows (can be either indoor or outdoor):
   a. Traditional recurve: 210
   b. Compound bow: 280
7. Visit an archery course and take part in an outdoor field round (28 targets). Attain the minimum scores using one of the following bows:
   a. Traditional recurve: 170
   b. Compound bow: 240

For additional resources, visit stren.life/archery.

ART BADGE

"In order to define art correctly, it is necessary to cease to consider it as a means to pleasure, and to consider it as one of the conditions of life. Viewed in this way, we see that art is one of the means of communication between man and man.

Every work of art causes the receiver to enter into a certain kind of relationship, both with the artist and all who receive the same impression. Just as words transmit thoughts, so art transmits feelings. The activity of art is based on the fact that when we witness a man experiencing an emotion, we to some extent share it. To evoke in oneself a feeling that one has once experienced, and to transmit that feeling to others through forms and colors, sounds or movements.

That is art. Art is not pleasure, but a means of union among men, joining them together in the same feelings, and indispensable for life and progress towards well-being of individuals and of humanity. Thanks to his capacity to express thoughts by

---

words, every man may know the debt he owes to the past, and be able to hand on what he has achieved to future generations. If humans lacked this capacity, we would be like wild beasts, and if people lacked this capacity for being infected by art, people might be more savage still, and more separated from one another."

–Leo Tolstoy

Philosophers have debated the meaning of art for centuries. Tolstoy certainly had a good theory on the subject. But whether you agree with it, or have your own, or aren't exactly sure how to define art, you probably have a craving to create it, even if the impulse may be very faint. In modern society, art is something everyone dabbles in as a child, a few grow up to pursue professionally, and most entirely abandon in adulthood.

But even if you put away your last watercolor set a long time ago, it's worth rediscovering your artistic side. Creating art combines feeling and imagination with technical skill and craft and offers a chance not only to communicate with others, but to express oneself; it provides an outlet for thoughts and emotions usually hemmed in by the banalities of one's workaday life. The ability to take that which exists, and create something wholly new—to produce beauty with one's own hands and agency—is one of the things that not only separates man from the beasts, but makes him close to the gods.

The Art Badge will help you access a bit of that divine power and take the first steps in enhancing your artistic skill. Even if your personal masterpieces are never worthy of hanging in a gallery, earning this badge will expand and enrich your interests and hobbies.

ART BADGE REQUIREMENTS

Complete all of the following requirements:

1. Visit 2 art galleries, museums, exhibits, etc.
2. Take a physical or online class in a medium of art you would like to learn. Class(es) must total at least 12 hours of instruction.
3. Create at least 4 pieces of art in the medium in which you took the class.
4. Create a piece of art you judge sufficiently worthy that you feel confident giving it to another person (besides your significant other) as a gift.

For additional resources, visit stren.life/art.

ASTRONOMER BADGE

"Astronomy compels the soul to look upward, and leads us from this world to another."

–Plato

Our ancient forbearers knew the night sky like the back of their hand. The constellations oriented them in a literal sense—as vital navigation tools—but in a spiritual one as well, serving as vivid reminders of their mythologies and place in the universe. Still today, knowing the constellations can be a source of essential survival skills (like orienting yourself with the North Star), satisfying knowledge, and humbling awe.

ASTRONOMER BADGE REQUIREMENTS

Complete 5 of the following requirements:

1. Observe and identify the phases of the moon over 1 full cycle; keep a log of your observations (if it's cloudy or

---

poor weather, note this, and also approximate what the moon phase is).

2. Identify the North Star, and know how to orient yourself towards the direction North with that knowledge; also know how to use the Big Dipper to identify the North Star. (In the Southern Hemisphere, identify the Southern Cross and know how to orient yourself towards South.)

3. Download and print star maps for your local night sky for the 4 seasons of the year. Then, identify in the night sky and without the help of aids, 5 constellations during each of the 4 seasons; explain the mythology behind the constellations to a friend.

4. Tell the hour of the night by the stars and the moon.

5. Know, name, and point out 3 of the planets.

6. Observe, with a friend or loved one, at least 1 annually-occurring meteor shower (even if it requires driving a distance into a rural area).

For additional resources, visit stren.life/astronomer.

BACKYARD CHEF

For millennia, cooking meat over a fire outside has been a nearly exclusive male activity. For example, in the traditional shepherd communities of Crete, women are responsible for most of the cooking, but if it's meat cooked outside, men do it. In Europe and America during the 17th and 18th centuries, barbecues in which whole pigs were roasted were a common community activity and men did the cooking.

With the Backyard Chef Badge, you'll tap into this timeless masculine tradition of cooking meat outside over a fire. By the time you complete the badge, you'll know how to both grill and smoke meat (almost) like a pro. Brace yourself. Your backyard will be the go-to place for summer parties.

BACKYARD CHEF BADGE REQUIREMENTS

Complete all of the following requirements:

1. Make a 3-zone fire and explain its benefits.
2. Detail the pros and cons of gas and charcoal grilling to a friend.
3. Grill hamburgers using charcoal.
4. Grill 4 of the following with either charcoal or gas:
   a. Steak
   b. Chicken
   c. Pork
   d. Fruit
   e. Vegetables
   f. Fish
5. Make your own seasoning rub *or* BBQ sauce.
6. Smoke 2 of the following meats:
   a. Brisket
   b. Pork ribs
   c. Pork butt

For additional resources, visit stren.life/backyardchef.

BACKYARD FARMER BADGE

In our modern world, we've become increasingly disconnected from our food. This isn't only true of our meat, but our produce as well. You can buy apples pre-sliced and you have likely encountered eggs exclusively in the context of styrofoam. We're entirely dependent on giant corporations to supply us with our sustenance.

The Backyard Farmer Badge will take you back to the land, even if that land is just a small garden box right outside your suburban house.

In starting a mini "farm," you'll find there's something extremely satisfying in watching a seed you planted grow into bonafide sustenance and in re-connecting the link between the food on your table and the life sources which provide it.

Plus, raising a food garden and/or food-producing animals will allow you to become more self-reliant, both in saving a bit of money on store-bought groceries, and having a back-up food supply should the SHTF.

BACKYARD FARMER REQUIREMENTS

Complete 4 of the following requirements:

1. Plant and harvest at least 3 vegetables suitable for your area.
2. Plant a fruit tree and harvest at least 3 pieces of fruit from it.
3. Plant and harvest one type of grain—barley, wheat, oat, etc.
4. Plant and harvest at least 3 different herbs.
5. Plant berry bush(es) and harvest at least one pint of berries from it.
6. Collect and save seeds from the vegetables and fruit you've harvested.
7. Create a compost pile and maintain it for at least 3 months.
8. Build a small chicken coop, raise chickens, and harvest eggs from it.
9. Build a rabbit pen and harvest rabbits for eating.

For additional resources, visit stren.life/backyardfarmer.

BARBELL BADGE

> *"A weak man is not as happy as that same man would be if he were strong. This reality is offensive to some people who would like the intellectual or spiritual to take precedence. It is instructive to see what happens to these very people as their squat strength goes up."*
>
> –Mark Rippetoe

In the past 20 or so years, fitness has gotten increasingly complicated. New training gizmos and programs have been developed promising to make you stronger and leaner.

But there's a form of training that's been time-tested for over a century and been proven to produce results: barbell training.

Barbell training is so simple, it's beautiful.

By utilizing just a few movements, you can get a full-body workout. No need for 20 different machines or fitness gizmos—all you need is a barbell and some plates. To

---

get stronger, you simply add weight in a controlled, progressive manner. That's it.

The best thing about barbell training is that it's humbling. It's you versus gravity. You can either lift the bar off the floor (or rack) or you can't. Henry Rollins put this clarifying quality of lifting masterfully:

> *"The Iron never lies to you. You can walk outside and listen to all kinds of talk, get told that you're a god or a total bastard. The Iron will always kick you the real deal. The Iron is the great reference point, the all-knowing perspective giver. Always there like a beacon in the pitch black. I have found the Iron to be my greatest friend. It never freaks out on me, never runs. Friends may come and go. But two hundred pounds is always two hundred pounds."*

BARBELL BADGE REQUIREMENTS

Complete all of the following requirements:

1. Perform the following lifts with exact form. Post a video in the Gymnasium for critique. If the feedback is mostly negative, fine-tune your technique, and re-post a video once you think you've got it:
   a. Low-bar squat
   b. Bench press
   c. Deadlift
   d. Shoulder press
   e. Power clean
   f. Clean and jerk
   g. Snatch

2. Follow a barbell training program (we recommend *Starting Strength*) until you can hit the following one-rep max benchmarks:
   a. Squat: 1.4x your bodyweight
   b. Bench press: 1x your bodyweight
   c. Deadlift: 1.7x your bodyweight
   d. Shoulder press: .7x your bodyweight
   e. Power clean: 1x your bodyweight
   f. Clean and jerk: .9x your bodyweight
   g. Snatch: .7x your bodyweight

For additional resources, visit stren.life/barbell.

BIOGRAPHY BADGE

"The best teachers of humanity are the lives of great men."

–Charles H. Fowler

Studying history, particularly the people who lived through it, greatly enlarges the palette of possibilities you can draw from when creating a vision for your own life. Only being aware of what you're surrounded with in the present is like living as a zoo animal, believing that your little artificial habitat is all there is to the world. But there are so many more ways to live. When you finish a great biography of a great man, your conception of what humanity is capable of broadens and your spirit feels perceivably expanded. You've caught a glimpse of alternative ways to earn a living, to structure your daily routine, to approach your relationships, to overcome setbacks, to have adventures, and to view the landscape of your life. The more biographies you read, the more you'll come to understand the world, the time period you're living in, yourself, and who you might become.

BIOGRAPHY BADGE REQUIREMENTS

Complete all of the following requirements:

1. Read 5 biographies.
2. Write a 500-1,000-word essay on what you learned from reading the biographies and post it in the Gymnasium.

For additional resources, visit stren.life/biography.

CITIZENSHIP BADGE

"In war you needed to have the man decent, patriotic, but, no matter how patriotic he was, if he ran away he was no good. So it is in citizenship; the virtue that stays at home in its own parlor and bemoans the wickedness of the outside world is of scant use to the community. We are a vigorous, masterful people, and the man who is to do good work in our country must not only be a good man, but also emphatically a man. We must have the qualities of courage, of hardihood, of power to hold one's own in the hurly-burly of actual life. We must have the manhood that shows on fought fields and that shows in the work of the business world and in the struggles of civic life."

–Theodore Roosevelt

Beginning with Ancient Greece, manliness in Western republics required being an active and engaged citizen. It was expected that each man do his part in ensuring the continued health and effective functioning of the government he lived under. This tradition continued throughout much of the 19th and early 20th centuries in democracies around the world. Men were charged with the duty of stepping "into the arena" and doing what they could to make their communities and countries stronger: being aware of national and local conditions and forming well-researched and well-reasoned opinions as to how they could be bettered, seeking justice, opposing corruption, voting regularly for who they believed to be the best candidate and the best cause, and disagreeing forcefully but civilly with their fellow citizens and elected lawmakers.

But as nation-states and cities have gotten bigger and more complex, and cynicism has calcified, civic engagement has decreased. Instead of getting their hands dirty with the workaday tasks that are necessary for good governance, most people opt to carp about the problems in their community and country online. Instead of being in the arena, we've settled for impotent rage and exhibiting what Theodore Roosevelt derisively called "parlor virtue."

The Citizenship Badge is designed to slough off the civic malaise that hangs upon many men today. While the badge explores citizenship at a national level, it's especially focused on local citizenship because that's where an individual's civic engagement can have the most immediate influence.

Will you answer TR's call to be "the man in the arena"?

CITIZENSHIP BADGE REQUIREMENTS

Complete 10 of the following requirements:

1. Read Theodore Roosevelt's "Citizenship in a Republic."

---

2. Read the founding documents of your nation. E.g., Americans would read the Declaration of Independence and the Constitution.
3. Read a book that provides a comprehensive big-picture view of your country's history.
4. Name all of your representatives at the national, state, and local level without looking them up.
5. Write or call one of your national, state, or local representatives about an issue important to you.
6. Attend a city council meeting. Introduce yourself to your councilor.
7. Attend a criminal trial.
8. Go on a police ride-along.
9. Volunteer 10 hours of your time to a local charity or service.
10. Regularly follow your local news for at least 10 minutes a day, for one month.
11. Visit a historical site that had a role in the history of your country.
12. Take a tour of your state capitol.
13. Vote in a local, state, or federal election.
14. Volunteer to campaign for a candidate you support.
15. Run for political office or volunteer to serve on a local board.

For required reading and additional resources, visit stren.life/citizen.

CLASSICS BADGE

We are the heirs of ancient Greece and Rome. Modern philosophy, science, literature, and government have all been influenced by ideas that originated in antiquity. Thus, to better understand our current world, it's necessary that we study the past from which it sprung.

What's more, many of our ideas of manliness and masculinity in the West come from ancient Greece and Rome. For the ancients, manhood was a mixture of courage, spiritedness, and physical and intellectual excellence. For most of Western history, cultures defined manliness in these classical terms. While we've turned away from this classical ideal of manliness in the 20th century, we still see vestiges of it today. Studying works from the classical era can thus help a man recapture and revive this ancient ideal of masculinity and apply it in his life.

The Classics Badge will expose you to a wide swath of classical culture. You will be doing a lot of reading for this badge; some works will take several weeks to finish, while others will take just a few hours. Don't rush yourself. Carve out space for contemplation and take as long as you need to complete this badge. Most of the reading can be found online for free, though we highly recommend buying new or used paperback versions for your own personal library. Highlight, take notes, and share what you've read with others.

CLASSICS BADGE REQUIREMENTS

Complete all of the following requirements:

1. Read 10 of the following works:
    a. *The Iliad* and *Odyssey* by Homer
    b. *Oedipus Rex* by Sophocles
    c. *The Oresteia* by Aeschylus
    d. *Medea* by Euripides
    e. *History of the Peloponnesian War* by Thucydides
    f. The following dialogues by Plato:
        i. *Laches*
        ii. *Meno*
        iii. *Phaedo*
        iv. *Crito*
        v. *Gorgias*
        vi. *Apology*
        vii. *The Republic*
    g. The following works by Aristotle:
        i. *Nichomechean Ethics*
        ii. *Politics*
        iii. *Rhetoric*
    h. Book VII of *Histories* by Herodotus
    i. *Aeneid* by Virgil
    j. The following works by Cicero:
        i. *De Officiis*
        ii. *De Senectute*
    k. *Odes* by Horace

1. The following works by Plutarch:
    i. *Spartan Lives and Sayings* found in *Parallel Lives*
    ii. *On the Education of Children*
    iii. *How to Tell a Friend From a Flatterer*
    iv. *How a Man May Become Aware of His Progress in Virtue*
    v. *On Chance*
    vi. *Can Virtue Be Taught?*
    vii. *On the Control of Anger*
    viii. *On Tranquility of Mind*
    ix. *On Love of Wealth*
    x. *On Envy and Hate*
  m. *Enchiridion* by Epictetus
  n. *Meditations* by Marcus Aurelius
  o. *On Tranquility of Mind* by Seneca
2. Write a 500-1,000-word essay on what you learned from your reading and post it in the Gymnasium.

For additional resources, visit stren.life/classics.

COMMUNITY SERVICE BADGE

"The service we render to others is really the rent we pay for our room on this earth. It is obvious that man is himself a traveler; that the purpose of this world is not 'to have and to hold' but 'to give and serve.' There can be no other meaning."

–Sir Wilfred Grenfell

Throughout cultures and history, to be a man required striving not just to take from your tribe, but to give back to it. To be a contributor and a creator, and not just a consumer. Men wanted to be on top back then, just as in every age, but part of earning esteem and honor required giving to those who had less and being irrationally generous with one's time, talents, and resources.

Unfortunately, today we live in a society that promotes an idea of manhood that's all about "getting mine." Self-interest entirely subsumes the interests of the group. We ask "What's in it for me?" instead of "What can I do to help?"

The irony is that by taking such a self-interested view towards life, we actually miss out on finding meaning and living a truly flourishing life. As Jesus and other wise men from antiquity noticed, whoever finds his life will lose it, and whoever loses his life will find it.

For the paradox of service is that while you're helping other people, you benefit greatly yourself—your perspective broadens, your gratitude and empathy increase, and your happiness and feelings of self-worth expand.

We all owe a debt to the society we live in. Don't just take from the pot—also put into it. Pay it back, and pay it forward, and you just might find that your own cup runneth over.

COMMUNITY SERVICE BADGE REQUIREMENTS

Complete the following requirement:

1. The requirements of this badge are simple, but not easy: Complete 30 hours of community service. How you decide to serve is up to you. Find a cause that's meaningful to you.

For additional resources, visit stren.life/service.

CRAFTSMAN BADGE

> *"The satisfactions of manifesting oneself concretely in the world through manual competence have been known to make a man quiet and easy."*
>
> –Matthew B. Crawford, Shop Class as Soulcraft

Across cultures and time, the archetype of the craftsman has represented man's ability to create and has been the mark of mature manhood. He is *homo faber* – man the creator. Instead of passively consuming and letting things happen to him, the craftsman fashions the world to his liking and proactively shapes and influences it.

There's a satisfaction that comes from making physical objects with your own hands that you can't get from anything else. The physicality of it gets you into a "flow" state and anchors your creativity in the real world. And when you're done crafting your object, you can see and touch it and share it with others. It has a tangible presence that more ethereal creative works like digital photographs or text on a computer screen can't match.

To help you experience the joys that come from being *homo faber*, we present the Craftsman Badge. Earning this badge will kick-start your journey to mastering materials with your own two hands.

CRAFTSMAN BADGE REQUIREMENTS

Complete all of the following requirements:

1. Read the AoM article "Measure Twice, Cut Once."
2. Read one of the following books:
   a. *Why We Make Things and Why It Matters: The Education of a Craftsman* by Peter Korn
   b. *Shop Class as Soulcraft* by Matthew Crawford
3. Choose and construct 3 objects from the list of possible projects below. You can choose to make all 3 projects in one medium (wood, leather, or metal), or make one in each medium, or a combination. You must post a photo of each of the completed crafts in the Gymnasium, and give one as a gift to someone.

Wood

- Shoeshine box
- Book shelf
- Ditty box
- Tie rack
- Tool box
- Birdhouse
- Key rack
- Dining room table
- Cribbage board

- Bench
- Cutting board
- Adirondack chair
- Simple box using wood joints (dowel, mortise and tenon, dovetail, etc.)
- Wine rack
- Candle holder

- Napkin holder
- Serving table
- Coffee table
- Night stand
- Gun case

- Grandfather clock
- Bedframe
- Pen
- Indian club
- Baseball bat

Leather

- Wallet
- Notebook cover
- Belt
- Tool roll-up case
- Dopp kit
- Valet tray
- Satchel
- Portfolio
- Moccasins

- Leather journal
- Watch strap
- Bracelet
- Gun holster
- Keychain fob
- Phone or tablet cover
- Axe, knife, or hatchet sheath

Metal

- Knife from an old saw blade
- Letter opener
- Flint and steel
- Ring from a quarter
- Coat hook
- Door knocker

- Candle holder
- Table
- Key holder
- Tent stakes
- Drawer handles
- Nails

For additional resources, visit stren.life/craftsman.

CRAFTSMAN BADGE

EASY RIDER BADGE

Few things have captured the passion—sometimes obsession—of men like the motorcycle. There's no mystery as to why this is. Motorcycles represent a peculiar combination of several manly elements: danger, speed, singular focus, solitude, mechanics, noise, and physical skill.

The Easy Rider Badge will help you get started down the path of learning how to ride a motorcycle safely and effectively so that you, too, can experience the joys of the wind blowing in your face while you cruise down an open road and into the sunset.

EASY RIDER BADGE REQUIREMENTS

Complete all of the following requirements:

1. Name the basic types of motorcycles and their features.
2. Name the basic parts of a motorcycle and their functions.

3. Explain the main and secondary controls of a motorcycle to a friend.
4. Demonstrate how to perform a pre-ride inspection.
5. Take a Basic Rider Course from an approved MSF Class.
6. Obtain your motorcycle license.
7. Read one of the following books:
   a. *Zen and the Art of Motorcycle Maintenance* by Robert Pirsig
   b. *Shop Class as Soulcraft* by Matthew Crawford

For additional resources, visit stren.life/easyrider.

EMERGENCY PREP BADGE

Most of our lives are pretty routine and boring. This consistency can lull us into a false sense of security. But every now and then, something happens that reminds us that there are forces out there we can't control—a fire starts in your home, a tornado rips through your neighborhood, the Blizzard of the Century blankets an entire region.

While we don't have control over these forces of nature, we can control how we respond to them. The Emergency Prep Badge will ensure that you're prepared for whatever life throws at you so that you can ride out a disaster.

EMERGENCY PREP BADGE REQUIREMENTS

Earn the following prerequisite badge:

1. First Aid Badge

Complete 4 of the following requirements:

1. Create a "Bug Out Bag" that will last you 72 hours in the event of an emergency.
2. Create a "Get-Home Bag" to stash in your car or place of work, or stock these emergency supplies in your car.
3. Create and document emergency plans for the following events that are applicable to your area; practice acting out an emergency drill in at least one of them:
   a. House fire
   b. Tornado
   c. Earthquake
   d. Hurricane
   e. Blizzard
   f. Power outage lasting more than 2 days
   g. Flood
   h. Wildfire
4. Know how to shut off the water, gas, and electricity in your house and why you'd need to do so in certain situations.
5. At a minimum, have a supply of food storage that would feed yourself and/or your family for 2 weeks.
6. At a minimum, store 14 gallons of water for each person in your home (this will be enough to last you 2 weeks in the event water services stop).

For additional resources, visit stren.life/prep.

EMERGENCY PREP BADGE

ENTREPRENEURSHIP BADGE

Back when your granddad or dad worked, they could stay with the same company for decades. For most modern workers, however, the days of spending one's entire career with the same company and retiring with a gold watch are long gone. Many men change jobs several times during their working life.

It's an uncertain time, but also an exciting one.

In order to thrive in our increasingly competitive and fast-changing economy, men today need to be a bit more flexible and self-reliant than their grandfathers or dads were. Instead of being "company men," they need to be entrepreneurial men. The Entrepreneurship Badge will help you gain the mindset and skill-set to become such.

Even if you don't plan on becoming fully self-employed, developing your entrepreneurial skills will still be beneficial. First, the skills necessary to start and run a successful business are skills big companies value. It's not enough to be able to simply follow orders—companies are also looking for individuals who can take initiative in starting and following through on projects that further the company's goals.

Second, having a small side hustle that brings in additional income is a crucial way of becoming "anti-fragile." The extra money you make from moonlighting can be used to pay down debt or can supplement your income if for whatever reason you lose your main job.

And who knows? Maybe you'll start a business that will become your full-time gig.

ENTREPRENEURSHIP BADGE REQUIREMENTS

Earn the following prerequisite badge:

1. Salesmanship Badge

Complete all of the following requirements:

1. Read 2 of the following books:
    a. *The $100 Startup* by Chris Guillebeau
    b. *Born for This* by Chris Guillebeau
    c. *The 7 Day Startup* by Dan Norris
    d. *Small Time Operator* by Bernard Kamoroff
    e. *The Personal MBA* by Josh Kaufman
2. Successfully start a side-hustle (business) by doing the following:
    a. Form an LLC for your business.
    b. Create a website to promote or sell your services or product.
    c. Earn $1,000 profit from your side hustle in a single month.

For additional resources, visit stren.life/hustle.

FIGHTER BADGE

The most obvious reason to learn how to fight is personal protection. But beyond this practical benefit exists several more metaphysical reasons to fight.

First, fighting—even within the controlled confines of the boxing ring—gives an individual a healthy appreciation of violence. Most people today experience violence vicariously through video games or movies. It's pretend and romanticized. They have no firsthand experience of the physical and emotional trauma actual violence can inflict. Contrast that with individuals who have actual experience with violence. They are more likely to say it should only be employed when absolutely necessary.

Second, physical fighting is a medium to help you withstand the mental and emotional blows that you'll experience in this life. "How much can you know about yourself if you've never been in a fight?" asks Tyler Durden, the protagonist in *Fight Club*. When you get in a physical fight and take that first punch in the nose and find yourself on the mat, it's in that moment you learn if you're the kind of man who gets back up after he's been knocked down. By giving and receiving physical kicks and punches you learn that pain is temporary and physical wounds heal. This knowledge bolsters your confidence outside the ring as well, endowing you with mental and emotional resilience.

Third, physical fighting can strengthen our moral compass and fortitude. Us moderns have a hard time accepting this idea and reconciling martial and moral virtues. We like to keep the two in separate mental compartments or act like they're fundamentally different. The ancients didn't see it that way—they understood that moral courage and physical courage were of the same essence, and that testing one's physical courage on the battlefield or in the sporting arena would in fact bolster their moral courage faster than a hundred "risky" intellectual or philosophical decisions. It's telling that Aristotle compared developing the philosophical mind to the boxer developing his physique and that the Stoics would often refer to soldiers and wrestlers as examples of their ideals.

Finally, fighting connects you with the very core of masculinity. So much of what makes men distinct from women—greater height, broader shoulders, higher testosterone—likely developed because of our role as fighters.

Vivere militare est—to live is to fight.

Are you prepared to live?

Then it's time to earn your Fighter Badge.

FIGHTER BADGE REQUIREMENTS

Complete the following mandatory requirement:

1. Become a member of a boxing, martial art, or MMA gym, and complete at least 24 hours of training/classes.

Complete 3 of the following requirements:

1. Read 2 of the following books:
   a. *The Professor in the Cage: Why Men Fight and Why We Like to Watch* by Jonathan Gottschall
   b. *A Fighter's Heart: One Man's Journey Through the World of Fighting* by Sam Sheridan
   c. *The Fighter's Mind: Inside the Mental Game* by Sam Sheridan
   d. *On Boxing* by Joyce Carol Oates
2. Demonstrate how to properly throw the following punches:
   a. Jab
   b. Straight punch
   c. Cross punch
   d. Hook punch
   e. Uppercut punch
3. Demonstrate the following Brazilian Jiu-Jitsu moves on a friend:
   a. Mount
   b. Guard position
   c. Bridge and roll mount escape
   d. Rear mount
   e. Guillotine choke
   f. Guillotine choke defense
   g. Triangle choke from guard
4. Using appropriate protective equipment, take part in a 3-round sparring session with a friend. Each round is 3 minutes long.
5. Earn at least the 3rd highest belt in a martial art.
6. Participate in an amateur boxing/martial art/MMA match.

For additional resources, visit stren.life/fighter.

FIRE BUILDER BADGE

"What is a camp without a campfire?—no camp at all, but a chilly place in a landscape, where some people happen to have some things.

When first the brutal anthropoid stood up and walked erect—was man, the great event was symbolized and marked by the lighting of the first campfire.

For millions of years our race has seen in this blessed fire, the means and emblem of light, warmth, protection, friendly gathering, council. All the hallow of the ancient thoughts, hearth, fireside, home is centered in its glow, and the home-tie itself is weakened with the waning of the home-fire. Not in the steam radiator can we find the spell; not in the water coil; not even in the gas log; they do not reach the heart. Only the ancient sacred fire of wood has power to touch and thrill the chords of primitive remembrance. When men sit together at the campfire they seem to shed all modern form and poise, and hark back to the primitive—to meet as man and

---

man—to show the naked soul. Your campfire part-
ner wins your love, or hate, mostly your love; and
having camped in peace together, is a lasting bond
of union—however wide your worlds may be apart.

The campfire, then, is the focal center of all primi-
tive brotherhood."

—*Ernest Seton, Manual of the Woodcraft Indi-*
ans, 1915

As Seton put it so well, fire has an almost magical quality.
It's highly utilitarian—it gives you heat and light that can
be crucial for survival. At the same time, its warm glow
seems to mysteriously build bonds and heighten one's experience in the wild.

To become a competent fire builder, you need to know
not only how to build a standard campfire with matches,
but how to build fire in a variety of circumstances, with a
variety of supplies, in a variety of ways.

FIRE BUILDER BADGE REQUIREMENTS

Complete 6 of the following requirements:

1. Make a fire using one of the following friction methods:
    a. Hand drill
    b. Bow drill
    c. Plough
2. Make a fire in rainy/wet conditions with only 2 match-
    es.
3. Make a fire without matches or friction method.
    May include:
    a. Magnifying glass

---

    b. Flint and steel

    c. Battery and steel wool

4. Build a teepee fire (using any method).

5. Build an upside down fire (using any method).

6. Build a reflector fire (using any method).

7. Build a cooking fire (using any method).

For additional resources, visit stren.life/fire.

FIRE BUILDER BADGE

FIRST AID BADGE

One of the greatest ways to serve your family, friends, and community is to always be ready to jump into a crisis and come to the assistance of those who may be injured and wounded. Whether you're tying a tourniquet on someone whose leg's been blown off by a bomb, or simply tending to your child's bee sting, first aid knowledge prepares you to offer comfort for minor emergencies, and possibly even save lives in big ones.

FIRST AID BADGE REQUIREMENTS

Complete the following mandatory requirement:

1. Take a First Aid/AED/CPR class.

Complete 6 of the following requirements:

1. Explain the symptoms and treatment for shock to a friend.

---

2. Explain the symptoms and treatment for snakebites to a friend.
3. Explain the symptoms and treatment for 2 different insect bites and stings to a friend.
4. Explain the symptoms and treatment for scalds and burns to a friend.
5. Explain the symptoms and treatment for poison ivy and poison oak to a friend.
6. Explain the symptoms and treatment for sunstroke, sunburn, and heat exhaustion to a friend.
7. Explain the symptoms and treatment for frostbite to a friend.
8. Explain the symptoms and treatment for convulsions and seizures to a friend.
9. Explain the symptoms and treatment for hypothermia to a friend.

Complete 5 of the following requirements:

1. Demonstrate how you would treat an open wound.
2. Demonstrate how to splint a fracture.
3. Buy/create a first aid kit for 1) your car, and 2) your home.
4. Demonstrate the correct use of a tourniquet and explain when one should/should not be used.
5. Demonstrate how to create a triangular sling.
6. Demonstrate ability to perform the fireman's carry.
7. Demonstrate ability to make an improvised stretcher (design of your choice).

For additional resources, visit stren.life/firstaid.

FIRST AID BADGE

FROGMAN BADGE

"He swims at all times, in rough water and against strong currents. When some day he is cast suddenly into the water at a disadvantage, wounded, it may be, or obliged to swim long under water in order to escape the enemy, he knows how to utilize his strength to the utmost, and often overcomes tremendous odds with the remarkable tact and skill of the Indian athlete." –Charles "Ohiyesa" Eastman (Sioux tribesman), Indian Scout Talks, 1915

Man is an amphibious animal, and knowing how to swim recreationally is a skill (and source of enjoyment) every man should possess. But it takes more than that to be a true frogman. To earn your Frogman Badge you'll not only have to be comfortable in the water, but be able to execute tactical maneuvers as well. You need to be able to swim underwater to avoid detection, retrieve something from the depths, save someone who's drowning, stay afloat, and more. You need to be able to maneuver in the water in a variety of elements and circumstances, whether you're in trunks in a pool or in clothes and carrying equipment in the open water. In short, to be a frogman, you've got to be able to swim skillfully for tactical, rescue, and survival purposes.

FROGMAN BADGE REQUIREMENTS

Complete 10 of the following requirements:

1. Swim 50 feet with shoes and clothes on (must be wearing pants, shirt, and closed-toe shoes).
2. Dive from the surface to 7-10 feet deep, and retrieve a weight of at least 10 pounds or more.
3. Take and pass the Navy SEAL Underwater Knot Tying Test.
4. Throw a rope to someone in the water who is at least 30 feet out from you, and pull them in.
5. Pull a person to shore by extending to them a pole, branch, oar, etc.
6. Perform a simulated water rescue (physically tow someone through the water to safety).
7. Swim 200 yards using good form, broken down by:
    a. Side stroke: 50 yards
    b. Backstroke: 50 yards
    c. Breast stroke: 50 yards
    d. Front crawl: 50 yards
8. Demonstrate the ability to turn either your pants or your shirt into an improvised flotation device.
9. Float as motionless as possible in water for 1 minute.
10. Enter water in complete silence, swim silently for 50 feet, leave water in complete silence. Have a friend present to give you a pass/fail.
11. Tread water while holding a brick in the following sequence: 30 seconds both hands in the water (with brick), 30 seconds right hand out of the water (with

brick), 30 seconds both hands in the water, 30 seconds left hand out of the water (with brick).

12. Tread water in clothes for 20 minutes.
13. Swim 25 feet underwater, taking a maximum of 2 breaths.
14. With any stroke, swim 1 mile in a pool or a half-mile in open water.

For additional resources, visit stren.life/frogman.

GEARHEAD BADGE

If you're like most men, you've probably taken your car to a pro for basic maintenance. While they can certainly get the job done quickly, you sometimes pay an arm and a leg for the service, and you don't end up learning anything about how your car works. With the Gearhead Badge, you'll learn how to do basic car maintenance jobs on your own, potentially saving you time and money, and certainly giving you a little more knowledge about a technology you use every single day, and the satisfaction that comes with working with your hands and being self-reliant.

GEARHEAD BADGE REQUIREMENTS

Complete 9 of the following requirements:

1. Read our Gearhead 101 Series.
2. Check the following fluids:
    a. Brake fluid
    b. Engine oil
    c. Coolant

    d.   Power steering fluid
    e.   Windshield washer fluid
    f.   Transmission fluid

3. Change the air filter.
4. Change the oil.
5. Change a tire.
6. Rotate your tires.
7. Change the windshield wipers.
8. Perform a radiator flush.
9. Replace a spark plug.
10. Replace the brake pads.
11. Replace the fuel filter.
12. Replace a headlight.

For additional resources, visit stren.life/gearhead.

GENTLEMAN
SCHOLAR BADGE

"Instruction ends in the school-room, but education ends only with life." –F. W. Robertson

For many men, once they leave formal schooling, their learning stops. But to live a truly flourishing life, one's education mustn't end once you say goodbye to the classroom. Every man, no matter his age or profession, must intentionally invest in, and take ownership of, the growth of his mind by becoming a gentleman scholar.

During the Renaissance and Enlightenment, gentleman scholars were men who had careers dedicated to things like farming or law, yet still continued to explore new topics, entertain fresh ideas, plumb intellectual horizons, and even make contributions to the world of knowledge. For example, Benjamin Franklin was a printer by trade, but he still managed to add to the science of optics and electricity in his spare time. Oh, and he also helped found a country, too.

Becoming a gentleman scholar, or learning how to learn by yourself, will expand your mind, open up new worlds of knowledge, make you more interesting and charismatic, and maybe even help you earn more money. If you're ready to start moonlighting as a perennial student, the Gentleman Scholar Badge will guide you on your auto-didactic journey.

GENTLEMAN SCHOLAR BADGE REQUIREMENTS

Complete all of the following requirements:

1. Read *Education of a Wandering Man* by Louis L'Amour.
2. Read chapters 1-4 of the *The Well-Educated Mind* by Susan Wise Bauer.
3. Take the Coursera Course "Learning How to Learn."
4. Listen to one lecture course of your choice from The Great Courses.
5. Take and complete an online course of your choice from either Coursera or edX on a topic you know little or nothing about.

For additional resources, visit stren.life/scholar.

HACKER BADGE

Our physical world has increasingly been eaten by the digital world. The way we're entertained, receive our news, and socialize is now primarily mediated by software.

It feels like magic to open up an app and have the information you want appear without you having to even think about it. Our software-driven world makes us feel like masters of our universe.

But what if the feeling of control and autonomy that software gives us is just an illusion?

Because if you step back and think about it, you're really not in charge. Software and apps have a logic and design that you're forced to work with and you didn't create those parameters, a computer programmer did. That wizard behind the curtain somewhere in Silicon Valley is the guy really in charge.

In today's digital world, the individuals who know how to program have gained increasing power not only financially (see Bill Gates), but also politically and socially. The rest of us non-programmers? We're just along for the ride.

Citizens of modernity either program or get programmed, so why not choose to climb into the driver's seat?

The Hacker Badge will help you gain a bit more autonomy in this software-eaten world we're living in. You probably won't be able to create the next killer app after you complete the badge, but you'll have a better understanding of the technology that's shaping us as individuals and as a society. And with that knowledge, you can take a more active (rather than passive) role in our brave new world.

HACKER BADGE REQUIREMENTS

Complete all of the following requirements:

1. Read *Program or Be Programmed* by Douglas Rushkoff.
2. Complete the HTML & CSS Course on Code Academy.
3. Complete the SQL Course on Code Academy.
4. Complete one of the following courses on Code Academy:
   a. PHP
   b. Python
   c. Ruby
5. Create one project using Arduino.

For additional resources, visit stren.life/hacker.

HANDYMAN BADGE

Grandpa's motto was "Use it up, wear it out, make it do, or do without." To follow this maxim in your own life, and make things last without having to pay money to a professional every time something breaks, you need to develop certain manual skills. Being able to repair and refurbish things around your house will not only save you money, but also give you the manly satisfaction of making things happen with your own two hands.

HANDYMAN BADGE REQUIREMENTS

Complete 10 of the following tasks:

1. Paint a door, wall, or ceiling.
2. Varnish a piece of furniture.
3. Solder something.
4. Hang a picture.
5. Repair broken blinds/hang new ones.
6. Lay new carpet.
7. Lay new tile.

8. Fix a leaky faucet or pipe.
9. Patch a hole in drywall.
10. Fix a window or door screen.
11. Replace an electrical outlet.
12. Replace a light fixture.
13. Repair a piece of furniture.
14. Replace a broken pane of glass.
15. Repair or build a fence.
16. Recondition/sharpen axe or garden tool.
17. Wallpaper a room.
18. Caulk cracks in shower/tub/window.
19. Weatherstrip a window/door.
20. Know location of the switch-offs for your main water, gas, and electric, as well as individual shutoffs for your major appliances.
21. Organize your garage.
22. Build a workbench.
23. Clear a clogged drain or trap.
24. Repair a broken toilet or install a new one.
25. Clean or replace a sprinkler head.
26. Build a wall.
27. Lay a walkway.

For additional resources, visit stren.life/handyman.

HOST BADGE

While throwing parties and social events is often seen as the responsibility of our female counterparts, men—particularly bachelors—have a long history of throwing memorable shindigs. The 1949 edition of *Esquire's Handbook for Hosts* states: "Granting that you are a bachelor and not a hermit...you are going to entertain pretty regularly in the apartment and not spend all of your time prowling after a pair of nylon legs."

Even if you're not a bachelor, being a host is a great way to practice your social skills, and exercise your capacity for creativity and generosity. Instead of passively waiting for good times to happen, you actively create memorable experiences for others. Instead of hoping to be invited to an event, you create the event yourself. Your friends are just as bored and lonely as you, so take the initiative in offering conversation, food, and drink, and bringing them out of the literal and metaphorical cold.

HOST BADGE REQUIREMENTS

Complete 5 of the following requirements:

1. Throw a dinner for 4+ guests.
2. Throw a holiday or birthday party for 10+ guests.
3. Hold a BBQ-type cookout for 4+ guests.
4. Host a poker/game night with 4+ guests; serve beverages and snacks.
5. Learn how to make 3 cocktails (can be alcoholic or non).
6. Host an overnight guest who stays for at least 3 days; help plan fun activities, and point them towards worthwhile sightseeing trips during their stay.

For additional resources, visit stren.life/host.

HUNTING BADGE

There are few activities as primal as hunting. It's been the main activity of man since the dawn of time. Today, it's a pursuit that's taken up by fewer and fewer men. But by earning the Hunting Badge, you're going to become one data point that runs in reverse of the trend.

Hunting immerses you in nature, teaches you the habits of wildlife, and inculcates qualities like patience and resilience; you're not going to bag game every time you go out—that's why they call it *hunting*, not *killing*!

But for this badge, you will have to keep getting out there until you take down an animal. And then you're going to eat it; instead of buying your meat pre-packaged in a styrofoam container, you're going to consume something you killed yourself, and finally participate directly in the circle of life.

HUNTING BADGE REQUIREMENTS

Complete all of the following requirements:

1. Take a hunter's safety course online and obtain your hunter certification for your state or area.
2. Plan and execute a hunting trip using either a bow or rifle:
    a. If it's your first hunt, find someone who's been hunting before to serve as your guide.
    b. Obtain a hunting license for the game you're hunting.
    c. Scout out the area you plan to hunt in.
    d. Successfully harvest and tag an animal.
3. Dress and clean the animal you harvested. Use the meat in a meal.

For additional resources, visit stren.life/hunting.

INFOSEC BADGE

In today's cyber-connected world, information is extremely valuable.

Information can give a company a competitive edge or topple governments. This is why governments and companies spend so much time and money on information security, or InfoSec for short.

As it goes with corporations and nation-states, so it goes with individuals. Your private information is a commodity to criminals and corporations. Your social security number in the hands of a criminal can allow him to take out large loans of money in your name. And your web surfing history can provide legitimate companies information to create targeted ads just for you.

In today's world, a man can't just be concerned about protecting his physical stuff. He needs to be concerned about protecting abstract information about himself too. Whether you want to protect yourself from criminal hackers and scammers or regain a bit of privacy from the government and corporations, the InfoSec Badge will help you do so.

INFOSEC BADGE REQUIREMENTS

Complete 10 of the following requirements:

1. Read 2 of the following books:
    a. *Social Engineering: The Art of Human Hacking* by Christopher Hadnagy
    b. *The Art of Deception: Controlling the Human Element of Security* by Kevin Mitnick
    c. *The Art of Intrusion: The Real Stories Behind the Exploits of Hackers, Intruders, and Deceivers* by Kevin Mitnick
    d. *Cybersecurity: Home and Small Business* by Raef Meeuwisse
    e. *Dragnet Nation* by Julia Angwin
2. Create a list of online accounts that contain information that would be devastating or damaging if compromised, which could include the following:
    a. Primary email account
    b. Online banking Account
    c. Amazon
    d. PayPal
    e. Dropbox
    f. iCloud
    g. Facebook
    h. Twitter
    i. Google accounts
    j. Online photo accounts
   For each of the accounts you list, do the following:
    - Create a different username for each account.
    - Use Diceware to create different passwords for each account.
    - Write new passwords in a physical notebook with no identifying information (username or which site the password is connected to). You'll come to

---

recognize which passwords belong to which accounts pretty quickly. Do not store them in your browser or on an online password manager.

- Enable two-step authentication for all accounts that allow you to do so.

3. Encrypt devices that you own that can store info that could be potentially devastating or damaging were it compromised. Ensure that you require login credentials to access your devices.

4. Install software on all your digital devices that will allow you to remotely clear and erase them in the event they are lost or stolen.

5. On your home WiFi system, use WPA2 and Diceware to create a password to access your WiFi. Install a firewall on your WiFi.

6. Create a "burner" email and phone number to use when companies or websites ask for these pieces of information.

7. Buy an external hard drive and back it up regularly—at least once a month for 6 months.

8. Install an anti-malware and adware program for your devices.

9. Delete your Google search history and tell Google to stop tracking your searches. Alternatively, delete your Google history and use the DuckDuckGo search engine exclusively for at least 2 weeks.

10. Install Ghostery on your browser so you can see what information a website is asking from your computer and decide whether you want to share that or not.

11. Perform a security audit on your online profiles. Remove any information that could possibly be used to get compromising information about you (birthday, birthplace, name of mother, name of best friend, phone number).

12. Remove any personal information that exists on the web about you (email address, home address, phone number).
13. Adjust settings on social media accounts (like Facebook), so that only people you personally know can see information about you.
14. Buy a paper shredder to dispose of mail that has potentially damaging information (bills, bank account statement, health insurance information, credit card statements), and use it for that purpose.
15. Buy a small safe to store any documents that could be used for identity theft (social security cards, passports, etc.).
16. Use annualcreditreport.com to get a free credit report to see if anybody has tried to open credit accounts in your name.
17. Sign up for a credit monitoring service.

For additional resources, visit stren.life/infosec.

JOURNALING BADGE

In studying the lives of great men, one of the most common themes you'll find is that many were avid journal keepers. Now, we won't say that the habit of journal writing is what made them great, but there's reason to think it helped.

Journaling provides myriad benefits. First, it helps you remember what was going on both internally and externally at certain points in your life. You always feel sure in the moment that you'll remember an experience forever. And yet even the most profound events fade with time. Being able to go back through old journals gives you a chance to revisit important milestones and even remember the ordinary day-to-day routines you once had, which become surprisingly interesting after the passage of time. And it offers you a window into how you've grown as a man (or perhaps stagnated).

Second, journaling can be therapy. Going through a rough spot in your life? Write about it. The act of writing—a highly analytical activity—forces you to be more rational about your negative emotions; it makes you step outside yourself and thus puts things into perspective. As you put pen to paper, you'll get insights as to how to solve a nagging problem or issue.

Finally, journaling is a tool in leaving your legacy. Sure, the environment your posterity will be living in will be different from yours, but they'll be dealing with the same problems: Disappointment. Thwarted ambition. Spurned love. Writing about those problems and how you dealt with them can provide comfort and insight to your posterity. And they'll just be plain interested to learn what everyday life was like at the beginning of the millennium.

The Journaling Badge requirements are simple, but the follow-through isn't. It requires steady dedication. Fortunately, after earning this badge, the journaling habit will be well-ingrained.

JOURNALING BADGE REQUIREMENTS

Complete all of the following requirements:

1. Complete the "Jumpstart Your Journaling 31-Day Challenge."
2. Write in your journal at least once a week for at least 8 weeks after finishing the Challenge.

For required reading and additional resources, visit stren.life/journaling.

KISS THE CHEF BADGE

While many of the world's great chefs are men, home cooking has often been seen as a feminine domain. This is unfortunate, as cooking is a skill that hones many manly qualities.

First, cooking is an important aspect of being a good host, as well as showing generosity and hospitality. Gathering people together to break bread strengthens relationships and builds community and tradition.

Second, like with any skill, it's a chance to gain mastery, engage in lifelong learning, and demonstrate curiosity and creativity; you can always be learning new techniques, experimenting with new dishes, and upping your culinary game.

Third, it provides a chance for adventure—whether you're hunting meat for your table, or for ingredients at a farmer's market, there's excitement in the pursuit of your next great meal.

Finally, cooking is an excellent way to practice the art of chivalry; women love a man who can cook, and regularly preparing your lady a delicious dinner or dessert is sure to

win her heart. Earn the Kiss the Chef Badge, and prepare
for an onslaught of smooches.

KISS THE CHEF BADGE
REQUIREMENTS

Complete 10 of the following requirements:

1. Make eggs 5 ways:
   a. Scrambled
   b. Poached
   c. Hardboiled
   d. Omelet
   e. Fried
2. Roast a chicken.
3. Make a pot roast.
4. Roast and carve a turkey.
5. Make a soup, stew, or gumbo involving at least 5 ingredients and 4 steps, where the majority of ingredients are from scratch.
6. Make a pasta dish involving at least 5 ingredients and 4 steps where the majority of ingredients are from scratch.
7. Make a dessert involving at least 5 ingredients and 4 steps, where the majority of ingredients are from scratch.
8. Make an appetizer where the majority of ingredients are from scratch.
9. Make/bake one of the following:
   a. Fresh pasta
   b. Sushi
   c. Homemade pizza dough
   d. Loaf of bread
   e. Beef jerky

10. Demonstrate proficiency with a kitchen knife:
    a. Properly chop an onion
    b. Properly mince a clove of garlic
    c. Properly dice a handful of herbs
11. Cook a 4-course dinner for at least 3 other people.
12. Cook a breakfast with at least 3 different dishes for at least 3 other people.

For additional resources, visit stren.life/chef.

KISS THE CHEF BADGE

KNOTSMANSHIP BADGE

For centuries, knot tying has been one of the handiest of essential man skills. Whether you're sailing the seas, climbing a mountain, or simply hauling lumber home, you need to know the right knot for the job, and how to tie it. A properly tied knot can mean the difference between losing a load of supplies, and even between life and death.

The Knotsmanship Badge will ensure that you know how to tie a trusty and true knot whenever the need arises.

KNOTSMANSHIP BADGE REQUIREMENTS

Complete all of the following requirements:

1. Tie the following knots without referencing any guides. Know when you'd use each:
    a. Square knot
    b. Figure eight knot
    c. Bowline

d. Two half hitches
  e. Clove hitch
  f. Sheet bend
  g. Taut-line
  h. Timber hitch
  i. Trucker knot
2. Tie the following lashings:
  a. Square lashing
  b. Diagonal lashing
  c. Shear lashing
3. Whip and fuse frayed rope ends.

For additional resources, visit stren.life/knots.

KNOTSMANSHIP BADGE

LETTER WRITING BADGE

Emails, texting, and the wide variety of other digital mediums available to us in the modern age are convenient and efficient, but they can't hold a candle to the warm, tangible, classy nature of handwritten correspondence. Letters are truly the next best thing to showing up personally at someone's door.

Of course, snail mail doesn't need to replace our digital messaging—it's just a satisfying activity (and even hobby, if you'd like) to take part in from time to time. It's nice to have a pen pal or two you correspond with through real letters; being able to open the mailbox and find an envelope addressed to you is a true delight.

Beyond basic correspondence, there are 7 types of letters every man should write at least once before he turns 70. Each kind of letter required for this badge covers a different part of the human experience, and provides a benefit to both the writer and the recipient (though you don't have to send them all). The former gets to participate in the exercise of putting words to feelings, a process that can hone gratitude, humility, and perspective on life. The

---

latter gets to open an envelope filled with comfort and encouragement. It's win-win.

With most of these types of letters, doing it once is definitely just the minimum goal. Making their writing a regular habit will keep the benefits flowing to you and the lucky recipients of your notes—until you're 70 and beyond.

LETTER WRITING BADGE REQUIREMENTS

Complete all of the following requirements:

For details of what these letters should consist of, read our article, "7 Letters to Write Before You Turn 70."

1. Write a letter of correspondence (a note just to say hello to someone, tell them what's been going on with you, and ask what's been going on with them).
2. Write a letter of congratulations.
3. Write a letter/note of condolence/sympathy.
4. Write a letter to your parent.
5. Write a letter to your future self.
6. Write a love letter.
7. Write a letter of encouragement.
8. Write a letter of gratitude.

For additional resources, visit stren.life/letters.

LOCK PICKER BADGE

There are a few good reasons why law-abiding citizens should learn how to pick a lock. First, it opens your eyes to the "illusion of security." Once you see how easy it is to pick a lock, you realize that while locks make us *feel* safe, if someone really wanted to get in your house, they could easily pick the lock on your front door. This will motivate you to utilize other tools and tactics and create multiple layers of security to keep you and your family safe.

Knowing how to pick a lock also makes you handy. If you've ever been locked out of your house or car, you know how annoying it is to be standing there like a chump, waiting for someone to show up with a key or a professional locksmith to arrive. Wouldn't you love to be able to jimmy your way in yourself? Not only can this skill save you a lot of time and money, being able to solve a problem like that on your own is pretty dang satisfying. Plus, you can help out all your friends when they get locked out too.

Finally, lock picking is just a cool skill to have. Of all the Jason Bourne-esque skills every man wishes he knew, it's one of the most attainable. The knowledge that you can surreptitiously enter most doors without a key will make you feel like some sort of super ninja-spy. It's also a fun little hobby. If you get really into it, you can actually go to events and contests to test your skills against other lock pickers.

LOCK PICKER BADGE REQUIREMENTS

Complete all of the following requirements:

1. Research and understand the legality of lock picking in your legal jurisdiction.
2. Pick a tumbler lock in less than one minute.
3. Pick a tumbler lock using picks made from a hairpin or paperclip.
4. Use a bump key to pick a tumbler lock.
5. Pick a tubular lock in less than one minute.
6. Pick a file cabinet lock in less than one minute.
7. Open a padlock with a soda can.

For additional resources, visit stren.life/lockpicker.

LUMBERJACK BADGE

The lumberjack represents a quintessential archetype of the strenuous life. Armed with his trusty axe and his hard-earned strength, he felled trees to provide pioneers with the wood they needed to build and warm log cabins, cook their food, and make the tools and products that would advance the nation. Today you can harness your inner lumberjack by choosing to provide yourself with the wood you need to heat your home, or simply build a cozy fireplace fire, and by having the know-how to be able to clear out fallen trees and debris after a storm or disaster.

LUMBERJACK BADGE REQUIREMENTS

Complete the following mandatory requirements:

1. Explain the basics of ax safety to a friend.
2. Explain the basics of chainsaw safety to a friend.

Complete 6 of the following requirements:

1. Identify 10 trees in your area.
2. Cut down a tree at least 6 inches in diameter with an ax or handsaw, demonstrating proper technique.
3. Buck a tree into logs with an ax.
4. Split at least 15 logs into firewood.
5. Sharpen an ax.
6. Fell a tree at least 6 inches in diameter with a chainsaw.
7. Buck a tree into logs with a chainsaw.
8. Sharpen a chainsaw blade.
9. Restore an heirloom ax.

For additional resources, visit stren.life/lumberjack.

LUMBERJACK BADGE

MICROADVENTURE BADGE

*"[Adventure] is a state of mind, a spirit of trying
something new and leaving your comfort zone. Adventure is about enthusiasm, ambition, open-mind-
edness, and curiosity...'adventure' is not only cross-
ing deserts and climbing mountains; adventure can
be found everywhere, every day, and it is up to us to
seek it out."*

–Alastair Humphreys, Microadventures

Do you have an itch for more adventure in your life?

Do you want to get out and explore more, but don't
have the time or money to undertake a major, globe-trot-
ting expedition?

Maybe this longing has made you feel frustrated
and stuck.

If that sounds like you, allow me to suggest earning the
Microadventure Badge.

The term "microadventure" was coined by Alastair
Humphreys, a true Adventurer with a capital A, who wanted to get people to think of adventure outside the big,

epic box we usually put the term in. Instead, he encourages folks to think small; rather than setting out on involved, far-flung expeditions, regularly take "microadventures"—tiny trips that butt right up against the boundary of what might be called an adventure at all, but still retain the fun, excitement, escapism, and challenge inherent to the essence of true adventures.

The beauty of microadventures is that they force you to throw out your usual excuses about why you can't live a more adventurous life: that you live in the suburbs, lack vacation time, have kids, don't have enough money, etc. Once you get going with them, you realize that adventures can be had close to home, fit into a 9-5 schedule, and don't require gobs of money, lots of gear, or special training.

The trick to busting through these imagined barriers is simply to start doing microadventures *consistently*, and this badge will help you do just that; earn it and you'll soon discover that small expeditions can pack a big punch.

MICROADVENTURE BADGE REQUIREMENTS

Complete all of the following requirements:

1. Read the following book and article:
    a. *Microadventures* by Alastair Humphreys
    b. "My 8-Week Microadventure Challenge"
2. Take an 8-Week Microadventure Challenge. For 8 consecutive weeks, you must undertake one microadventure per week. The microadventure must last at least one hour, but what it consists of is up to you. Consult the book and article above for ideas, and use the below websites for help in finding little adventures in your backyard:
    a. theoutbound.com/

b. roadsideamerica.com/location
c. roadtrippers.com
d. alltrails.com

For required reading and additional resources, visit stren.life/adventure.

MONK BADGE

Culturally, we're very familiar with the idea of training the body. We think less, however, of training the *soul.*

Yet the health of both "physiques" requires the same kind of dedicated, intentional effort; indeed, both the body and the spirit atrophy from lack of use, increase in strength and agility when exercised, require pain, weight, and opposition to grow, and can only be honed through consistent, continual practice.

The body is trained through exercises like running and lifting weights; the soul is trained through exercises called the "spiritual disciplines." Regular practice of these disciplines does not require secluding oneself in a cloister, but can, with commitment, be accomplished amidst the hustle and bustle of the modern, workaday world. Practice of the disciplines will allow you to carve out a monastic current in your life: a quiet, sacred chamber in one's heart that brims with peace, solitude, wisdom, and true spiritual power, regardless of circumstances.

Completion of the Monk Badge will help you to access a higher plane of existence, while living in a frantic, shallow, existentially enervated landscape.

MONK BADGE REQUIREMENTS

Complete all of the following requirements

1. Read the Art of Manliness' Spiritual Disciplines series.
2. Study a religious or philosophical text using at least 2 techniques of your choice from those suggested in the Study section of "The Spiritual Disciplines: Study and Self-Examination," for at least 10 minutes a day for 30 consecutive days.
3. Practice one of the self-examination practices outlined in the Self-Examination section of "The Spiritual Disciplines: Study and Self-Examination" every day for 30 consecutive days.
4. Spend 90 minutes in solitude a week for 8 consecutive weeks. It is not required that you do the 90 minutes in one uninterrupted block; you can divide the time up and get in snatches at different times/days. For the purposes of this requirement, solitude is defined as:
   - If indoors, you must be in an enclosed space (room, office, closet, vehicle) in which no other person is present.
   - If outdoors, no other human beings can be in your line of sight (should they wander into it unexpectedly, that is okay).
   - The time/space must be free of human-created noise/input (no reading/internet surfing/listening to music; an environment as free from unnatural ambient noise as possible)
   - While showers can ordinarily serve as a time of solitude, for the purposes of this requirement, they do not count towards your 90 minutes.
5. Fast from food and caloric beverages (black tea and coffee and diet soda are okay) for 24 hours at least once a month for 3 months.

6. Write out your life's purpose. Hang it somewhere where you will see it often.
7. Successfully abstain from a habit that keeps you from better prioritizing your life's purpose for 30 days.

For required reading and additional resources, visit stren.life/monk.

MONK BADGE

MOUNTAIN RANGER BADGE

*"The Gods of the Hills
are not the Gods of the Valleys."*

–Ethan Allen

"Higher."

*–Motto of the 86th Regiment,
10th Mountain Division*

Mountains make up about 1/5 of the earth's landscapes, and represent one of nature's most compelling and challenging terrains. Men have always been drawn to the mountains, humbled by their mighty, soaring peaks, captivated by the ancient mystery they seem to bespeak, and inspired by the chance they offer to climb towards the heavens.

Men continue to hear the call of the mountains today, and it takes a different skill-set to navigate their diverse terrains than it does the lowlands. You need to be comfortable scrambling over rocks, scaling cliffs, and traversing through snow. The Mountain Ranger Badge will get you familiar with all these domains, so that you may ascend and descend from on high.

MOUNTAIN RANGER BADGE REQUIREMENTS

Complete 8 of the following requirements:

1. Climb at least 2 mountains that are at least 3,500' in elevation.
2. Climb at least one mountain 14,000' or more in elevation.
3. Take a ski class (minimum 3 hours).
4. Take a rock climbing class (minimum 3 hours).
5. Snowshoe for 30 miles (non-consecutive).
6. Ski down at least 6 different black diamond ski runs.
7. Make a 400-foot vertical ascent and descent on skis under complete control with a pack of at least 15 pounds.
8. Cross-country ski 200 miles (non-consecutive).
9. Rappel down at least 5 rock faces that are at least 100' high.
10. Spend 30 hours ice or rock climbing and/or bouldering (non-consecutive).
11. Take an avalanche safety course.
12. Build a snow shelter and sleep in it overnight.
13. Explain to a friend how to treat frostbite and hypothermia.

For additional resources, visit stren.life/mountain.

MUSIC BADGE

"God has given us music so that above all it can lead us upwards. Music unites all qualities: it can exalt us, divert us, cheer us up, or break the hardest of hearts with the softest of its melancholy tones. But its principal task is to lead our thoughts to higher things, to elevate, even to make us tremble... The musical art often speaks in sounds more penetrating than the words of poetry, and takes hold of the most hidden crevices of the heart...Song elevates our being and leads us to the good and the true."
–Friedrich Nietzsche

The Mustachioed Philosopher was right.

Music stirs the soul.

A single song can fill our spirits with *thumos* or evoke sweet memories of loved ones passed on. Singing or performing with a group of people, and sharing in these feelings together, can be uniquely unifying, and make us feel connected to something larger than ourselves.

Sadly, most folks today only scratch the surface of music's awesome power. And they constrain themselves in two ways. First, they limit their musical exposure to a set genre or whatever is popular at the moment. In this they deny themselves from experiencing the rich tapestry of music that's been created across culture and time.

Second, they are mere spectators when it comes to music. Instead of singing or playing their own music, they passively watch others, usually professionals. But there's power in taking an active part in the creation of music. Performing it—whether singing a song or playing an instrument—connects the body with the spirit and the spirit with community in a very visceral way.

The Music Badge aims to help you remedy your musical deficiencies by exposing you to a wide variety of great music as well as getting you started in participating in music yourself.

MUSIC BADGE REQUIREMENTS

Complete 5 of the following requirements:

1. Listen to at least an hour of 5 of the musical styles below; choose styles you have not listened to in the last year:

   a. Gregorian chant
   b. Madrigal
   c. Renaissance mass
   d. Baroque opera
   e. Baroque oratorio
   f. Baroque concerto
   g. Lutheran Cantata
   h. Classical era (Mozart, Beethoven, Joseph Haydn, Bach, Handel, Vivaldi)
   i. Romantic opera (Verdi, Wagner)
   j. Romantic symphony (Chopin, Brahms, Tchaikovsky, Rachmaninoff, etc.)
   k. Symphonic modernism (Debussy, Stravinsky, Schonberg)
   l. Blues
   m. Gospel

n. Ragtime
o. New Orleans jazz
p. Chicago jazz
q. New York jazz
r. Swing
s. Bebop
t. Cool
u. Modal jazz
v. Bluegrass
w. Celtic

x. Western swing
y. Rockabilly
z. Funk
aa. Rock
ab. Hip-hop
ac. Scottish folk music
ad. Japanese folk music
ae. Native American
af. Reggae

2. Attend a live performance of 2 of the musical styles listed above; the 2 concerts must be of a musical style you've never attended a concert for.
3. Create a playlist of music that inspires and moves you.
4. Explain to a friend the following about sheet music:
   a. The notes on the treble clef
   b. The notes on the bass clef
   c. The value of different note symbols
   d. The value of different rest symbols
   e. Time signature
5. Sing a song or hymn from a music sheet with good melody, pitch, rhythm, and tone in front of another person.
6. Sing a song with 2 or more people. Let the others sing tenor, while you sing bass.
7. Spend at least 24 hours participating in a church or community choir.
8. Spend at least 24 hours learning how to play a musical instrument (may be either classes or self-study).
9. Play 2 songs on the instrument of your choice in front of another person.
10. Spend at least 24 hours playing an instrument in a band or orchestra.

For additional resources, visit stren.life/music.

MUSIC BADGE

ORATOR BADGE

For most of Western history, men were trained in the art of oration. A well-educated and involved citizen was expected to write and speak effectively and persuasively and students devoted several years to studying how to do so.

But in the early part of the 20th century, a shift in education occurred. Degrees which prepared students for specific careers replaced a classical, liberal arts education. Today's college students often get only a semester of rhetoric training in their Freshman English Composition classes and these courses often barely skim the subject (if it's covered at all).

Which is quite unfortunate.

Our economy and society are becoming increasingly knowledge and information based; the ability to communicate effectively and persuasively is more essential to success than ever before. And being able to say a few poignant, heartwarming, or witty words that touch hearts and enhance an occasion is central to being a consummate gentleman.

If you got short-shrifted in the public speaking department growing up, the Orator Badge is here to help. You'll learn how to address an audience no matter the situation, whether it's making a pitch to a client, accepting an award, or proposing a toast.

ORATOR BADGE REQUIREMENTS

Complete 5 of the following requirements:

1. Read or listen to 5 of the speeches listed in our article, "The 35 Greatest Speeches in History."
2. Read 2 of the following books/articles on public speaking:
   a. *How to Develop Self-Confidence & Influence People by Public Speaking* by Dale Carnegie
   b. *Rhetoric 101* by Brett and Kate McKay
   c. *The Art of Public Speaking* by Stephen Lucas
   d. *Talk Like TED* by Carmine Gallo
3. Deliver a 3-minute impromptu speech on a topic randomly selected by a friend, to an audience of at least 5 people.
4. Prepare and deliver a 5-minute speech that informs an audience of at least 5 people about an object, process, event, or concept.
5. Prepare and deliver a 10-minute speech that persuades an audience of at least 5 people about a question of fact, value, idea, or policy. When you are finished, ask the audience for honest feedback on the following criteria; video the speech and critique yourself later as well:
   a. Voice pitch
   b. Rate of delivery
   c. Articulation
   d. Vocal variety
   e. Hand gestures
   f. Eye contact with audience
   g. Posture

6. Prepare and deliver a 5-minute presentation using a visual aid (like PowerPoint) to an audience of at least 5 people. When you are finished, ask the audience for honest feedback on the following criteria; video your delivery and critique yourself as well:
    a. Visual aid was only displayed while discussing it.
    b. Talked to audience and not visual aid.
    c. Visual aid is simple and easy to read.
7. Make 2 of the following speeches:
    a. Wedding toast
    b. Eulogy
    c. Dinner/birthday/New Year's Eve toast
    d. Introductory speech for another speaker or notable guest
    e. Accepting an award
    f. Giving an award

For required reading/listening and additional resources, visit stren.life/orator.

OUTDOORSMAN BADGE

"Everybody needs beauty as well as bread, places to play in and pray in where nature may heal and cheer and give strength to the body and soul. Keep close to Nature's heart...and break clear away, once in awhile, and climb a mountain or spend a week in the woods. Wash your spirit clean."

–John Muir

For thousands of years, nature was not something to visit, or paint, or photograph, but man's home, as inseparable from his existence as water is to a fish. Today, we spend most of our time in fluorescent-lit, climate-controlled buildings, and this disconnect from our natural habitat takes a toll on our mental and physical health. Research shows that immersing yourself in nature is good for body, mind, and soul, lowering one's chances of obesity and depression, and boosting mental sharpness, calmness, immunity, and even testosterone. Time spent in nature also has a bevy of unquantifiable but undeniably real and potent effects: humbling you as to your transience and vul-

nerability, heightening your senses and creativity, center-
ing your mind, and opening your spirit to feelings of flow,
peace, and spirituality.

The great outdoors is one of the best places to practice
The Strenuous Life, and many of the skills and aptitudes
you'll develop through other badges in the TSL program:
hike a mountain, make a campfire, catch a fish, navigate
with a map, set up your tent with well-tied knots, track
animals, etc. But it's also a place to explore with no agen-
da at all, besides reconnecting with the basic, primal elements of life.

In stripping off the patina of civilization, and loosening
the collar of rules and routine, a man's spirit is rejuvenat-
ed and his vigor restored. By getting lost in nature, you
may find the answers to questions you've been asking, and
come back to yourself.

The requirements of this badge are simple, because we
really want to get you outdoors—regularly and frequently!

OUTDOORSMAN BADGE
REQUIREMENTS

*Complete all of the following requirements, beginning when
the badge is commenced, and completed within 1 year:*

1. Camp 14 days and nights (non-consecutive) in a tent or
    in the open.
2. Hike 100 miles (non-consecutive).

For additional resources, visit stren.life/outdoorsman.

OUTDOORSMAN BADGE

PATER FAMILIAS BADGE

Have you ever met one of those families that just seem to have it all together? Maybe you knew such a family growing up and loved hanging out over at their house—there was such a great atmosphere there that you kind of felt like you were coming home whenever you stopped over. The parents were happy. The kids were all well-adjusted and generally did the right thing. Everyone in the family seemed to genuinely love, respect, and care about each other. Sure, they had problems and struggles like any other family, but they supported each other and rallied together to take care of whatever they were going through.

If you ask those families the secret to happiness, they all pretty much say the same thing: they're *intentional* about creating and fostering a positive family culture.

Whether you know it or not, your family is always creating a culture within itself. Culture is how you all work together toward common goals. It's made up of spoken and unspoken values, norms, and traditions.

If you want a family that's thriving and flourishing, you have to be intentional about shaping your family's culture. You can't just leave it to chance. You have to be a leader in your home, and guide your family towards shared values and goals.

The Pater Familias Badge will help you father and husband with more intentionality so you can have the kind of home life you've always wanted.

PATER FAMILIAS BADGE REQUIREMENTS

Complete the following mandatory requirement:

1. Read the following books/article series:
    a. *Do Fathers Matter: What Science is Telling Us About the Parent We Overlooked* by Paul Raeburn
    b. *The Secrets of Happy Families* by Bruce Feiler
    c. "Creating a Positive Family Culture" by Brett and Kate McKay

Complete 3 of the following requirements:

1. Lead and hold a Family Meeting once a week for 8 consecutive weeks.
2. Hold a Marriage Meeting once a week for 8 consecutive weeks.
3. Along with your family, create a family mission statement. Display it prominently somewhere in your home.
4. Create a new family tradition you can do monthly, and take part in it for 3 consecutive months.

For required reading and additional resources, visit stren.life/family.

PENMANSHIP BADGE

Penmanship may be a dying art, but it remains a pursuit well worth mastering. Writing things out by hand has been shown to help improve learning, adds a personal and emotional touch to your correspondence, and is the most fail-proof way to take notes on the go—no batteries or electricity required!

This badge concentrates on cursive penmanship as it not only begets these benefits, but has ones of its own: writing in cursive is meditative, easy on the hand, and best of all just looks darn classy.

PENMANSHIP BADGE REQUIREMENTS

Complete all of the following requirements:

1. Demonstrate the ability to hold a pen correctly when writing in cursive.
2. Demonstrate the proper way to position your paper for optimal writing.

---

3. For 15 consecutive days practice penmanship movement exercises for 5 minutes (exercises found on the badge resource page, listed below).
4. For 15 consecutive days practice writing the entire alphabet.
5. In your best cursive handwriting copy 3 of the following poems and excerpts:
    a. "If" by Rudyard Kipling
    b. "The Man in the Arena" by Teddy Roosevelt
    c. "In a Far Country" by Jack London
    d. "The Joy of Doing" by Raymond John Baughan
    e. "Invictus" by William Ernest Henley
6. Send a handwritten letter to 3 friends or loved ones.

For required exercises and additional resources, visit stren.life/penmanship.

PENMANSHIP BADGE

PERSONAL FINANCE BADGE

Thrift, simplicity, self-sufficiency, and the ability to prudently manage resources have long been important virtues, as they allow a man to not only maintain his autonomy and liberty, and take care of those he loves, but to also maximize his chances of progress; mastery of personal finance isn't just a defensive move—protection against want—but a skill that sets you and your family up for being able to take advantage of the greatest number of opportunities.

Unfortunately, most men never got a proper education on personal finance. We're expected to pick up this vital know-how on our own. With the Personal Finance Badge, you'll get some much needed direction in the sometimes overwhelming area of money so that you can lay a foundation for financial security and success.

PERSONAL FINANCE BADGE REQUIREMENTS

Complete 7 of the following requirements:

1. Read 2 of the following books on personal finance:
   a. *Total Money Makeover* by Dave Ramsey
   b. *I Will Teach You to Be Rich* by Ramit Sethi
   c. *Get a Financial Life: Personal Finance in Your Twenties and Thirties* by Beth Kobliner
   d. *Bogleheads' Guide to Investing*
   e. *Your Money or Your Life* by Joe Dominguez and Vicki Robin
2. Create a list of 5 financial goals for the next 5-10 years of your life.
3. Track your spending using an expense tracker for at least 60 days (we recommend Mint).
4. Create a debt repayment plan.
5. Save at least $1,000 in an emergency fund.
6. Create a monthly budget.
7. Reduce one of your monthly budget expenditures by 10%.
8. Check your credit score and report.
9. Open a retirement account using one of the following methods, and set aside a portion of your monthly income to it (at least 5% for 6 months):
   a. Use your company's 401k.
   b. Open a Roth IRA account.
   c. If you're a small business owner, open a SEP IRA.
10. Negotiate the price down for a large purchase.
11. Pay off your debt (all except mortgage).

For additional resources, visit stren.life/finance.

POLYGLOT BADGE

For centuries, learning multiple foreign languages (often at least one ancient language and a few modern ones) was a requisite part of the gentleman's education. Today, while students ostensibly get taught a second language in high school and college, without regular practice, most adults forget just about everything they learned and can only speak their mother tongue.

But knowing a second (or third, or fourth) language can really open up a literal and metaphorical world of opportunities. When you know the native language of a country you visit, you can have a deeper and more immersive experience there, as you're able to interact with locals and read the texts and better understand the art their culture has produced. When you know another language, you can talk with foreign visitors to your own country. It can also advance your career; knowing another language in an increasingly globalized world can put you ahead of the pack, and increase your salary to boot. Additionally, learning another language has been shown to increase your smarts as a whole; bilingual folks score higher on tests than monolinguals, especially in the realms of math, reading, and writing. Finally, being a polyglot is simply satisfying: learning a foreign language stretches the mind, talking to others in your non-native tongue feels risky and fun, the skill adds an element to your confidence and *savoir faire*, and the knowledge makes you more of a man of the world.

POLYGLOT BADGE REQUIREMENTS

Complete all of the following requirements:

1. Complete a course in a foreign language on Duolingo, Babbel, or busuu.
2. Using the foreign language you learned, take part in a 30-minute conversation with someone who is a fluent speaker in that language.
3. Read a 100+ page book in this foreign language.
4. Write a 1,000 word essay on the topic of your choice in this foreign language.
5. Translate a poem from your native tongue to this foreign language.
6. Watch a film in this foreign language.

For required reading and additional resources, visit stren.life/polyglot.

ROUGH RIDER BADGE

There's a reason Theodore Roosevelt is the patron saint of The Strenuous Life. He coined the phrase and embodied living life "in the arena" like no other figure in history. He was a true renaissance man who loved to do difficult things, had a wide array of interests, and managed to circumscribe the hard virtues like physicality and courage, with softer qualities like intellectual curiosity and compassion.

In seeking to always to live the strenuous life, he managed to do all the following, and much more, during his 60 years on earth:

- Worked as state legislator, police commissioner, and governor in New York.
- Owned and worked a ranch in the Dakotas.
- Served as Assistant Secretary of the Navy.
- Fought as a Rough Rider in the Spanish-American War.
- Served as President for two terms, then ran for a third.
- Became the first President to leave the country during his term in order to see the building of the Panama Canal.

- Wrote 35 books.
- Read tens of thousands of books—several a day, in fact, and in multiple languages.
- Discovered, navigated, and then named a completely uncharted Amazonian river over 625 miles long.
- Earned the Nobel Peace Prize and the Medal of Honor (posthumously).

While no one will ever likely achieve what Roosevelt did, every man can learn more about his remarkable life and do a few things to follow in his footsteps and capture the vigorous spirit of the Bull Moose.

ROUGH RIDER BADGE REQUIREMENTS

Complete 6 of the following requirements:

1. Learn more about Roosevelt's life by reading:
    a. Edmund Morris' trilogy of biographies on Theodore Roosevelt
    b. Theodore Roosevelt's own autobiography
2. Absorb the conviction to live the strenuous life into your sinews by memorizing the "Man in the Arena" quote.
3. Roosevelt passionately advocated for every man remaining physically vigorous throughout his life. To see if you're hearty and ready for action, complete the challenge he issued to Marines: Walk 50 miles in 20 hours.
4. Roosevelt became an amateur natural historian as a boy and retained his interest in the subject throughout his life. As such, you should:
    a. Identify the sound of three birds in your area.
    b. Visit a natural history museum.

    c. Go out in nature and make 3 sketches of flora and fauna.
5. Roosevelt took up boxing and jiu-jitsu—spark your pugilistic spirit by taking at least one boxing or martial arts class.
6. Roosevelt invigorated himself by skinny-dipping in the Potomac River; do likewise by taking a dip in the buff in a natural body of water outside of the months of summer.
7. Roosevelt was a voracious reader; follow in his footsteps and get a taste of the texts that influenced his mind by choosing and reading 3 books from his recommended reading list.

For required reading and additional resources, visit stren.life/roughrider.

RUCKING BADGE

Rucking is simple.

Put some weight in a backpack and go for a walk.

That's it.

But don't let the simplicity of rucking fool you. With some creativity, you can make rucking one of the hardest physical challenges you've ever done.

It's a fantastic way to get in an extremely functional cardio and strength workout. You don't just have to walk with your ruck—take it off and press it up in the prone position, or wear it while doing push-ups and other calisthenics. If you ever find yourself having to hike for miles in the wilderness with a heavy pack, rucking will have prepared you for it. Going to spend a day lifting and carrying heavy bags of mulch? It will be a breeze after a few weeks of rucking.

One of the best things about rucking is that it's an exercise that can get you out into nature. There's something very satisfying about hiking through a local wilderness area for an hour or two, soaking in the sun and the relaxing sounds of the woods, all while hoisting a 45-pound ruck on your back.

To increase the feel-good effects of rucking, bring along a bud or 8 for a dose of social medicine.

Then, when you're ready to take your rucking to the next level, sign up for a GoRuck Challenge. This 12-hour event will push you beyond your mental and physical limits as well as teach you how to work better as a team.

Long live rucking.

RUCKING BADGE REQUIREMENTS

Complete all of the following requirements:

1. Explain to a friend how to take care of your feet during a ruck/march/hike.
2. Ruck one hour a week with a 40-pound weight, for 4 consecutive weeks.
3. Ruck with a 40-pound weight for 50 miles over 48 hours.
4. Complete a GoRuck Challenge.

For additional resources, visit stren.life/rucking.

SALESMANSHIP BADGE

We often think of salesmanship as being a skill only necessary to individuals who work in careers where the primary job description is selling—car salesman, ad salesman, etc. But the reality is, we're ALL salesmen. When you make a business pitch, you're selling. When you take part in a job interview, you're selling yourself. When you negotiate a bill down, you're selling. As author Daniel Pink noted, anytime we're trying to move others to exchange what they have (be it money, time, energy, commitment) for what we have, we're selling. And in an increasingly competitive economy, the ability to persuade others to go with your product or service has become an increasingly valuable skill.

The ability to sell isn't just relegated to the market, either. If selling is about persuasion, then you engage in selling all the time with your friends and family too. Asking a woman on a date? You're pitching yourself. Trying to convince your kid to get off the computer and go outside? Selling.

The Salesmanship Badge will get you started down the path of becoming a master persuader. Selling isn't about bulldozing people with overbearing pitches. It's about figuring out their needs and creating a compelling story that demonstrates how you can fulfill them.

SALESMANSHIP BADGE REQUIREMENTS

Complete 7 of the following requirements:

1. Read 2 of the following books:
    a. *To Sell Is Human* by Daniel Pink
    b. *Influence: The Psychology of Persuasion* by Robert Cialdini
    c. *Never Split the Difference* by Chris Voss
    d. *Made to Stick* by Chip and Dan Heath
    e. *Pitch Anything* by Oren Klaff
    f. *Starting With No* by Jim Camp
2. Create a list of at least 10 of your favorite TV, internet, magazine, or other types of ads. Write down what you liked about these pitches. Did they persuade you to buy the product or service, or to remember their name? If so, how did they do it?
3. Develop and deliver a compelling 5-minute pitch to a friend or family member about a plain No. 2 pencil. Resolve doubts that your friend has about making the purchase by focusing on the needs of the buyer.
4. Develop a one-sentence pitch expressing the talent and skill you bring to your business or the business you work for. Focus on answering the following questions in your pitch:
    a. What do you want them to know?
    b. What do you want them to feel?
    c. What do you want them to do?
5. Create a "Pixar Story" Pitch that makes the case on why you should get a raise. Use the following format:

"Once upon a time _____ . Every day, _____ .
One day _____ . Because of that, _____ . Because of that, _____ . Until finally _____ ."
(from Daniel Pink, *To Sell Is Human*)

6. Compose a compelling pitch for an organization, church, club, or hobby you participate in, in the form of a tweet (140 characters) you think would convince others to try it.
7. Successfully persuade a family member/friend/associate to donate money to a charity of your choice.
8. Successfully negotiate the price down for a product you're buying, or your credit card, cell phone, or internet/cable rate.
9. Successfully sell someone something worth at least $100.

For additional resources, visit stren.life/sales.

SARTORIALIST BADGE

In modern times, caring about how you dress has sometimes been criticized as superficial or shallow—the purview of men who try too hard and who are "artificial."

But this attitude is a recent phenomenon, a blip in the stretch of history. Men have in fact cared about how they dressed since time immemorial; even primitive men, who had very little in the way of material to work with, found ways to get gussied up for special events, feeling that donning certain ceremonial ornaments and body paint contributed to their own enjoyment, as well as the overall drama and significance of rituals and celebrations. In the centuries since, men took great care in their clothing choices, knowing that their get-ups would communicate volumes about their personality and status, and wanting to show respect to others. They saw no conflict between being men of deep character, doing practical, rough-n-tumble deeds, and caring about how they looked.

Still today, you should know how to dress for reasons both self-serving and altruistic. When you dress well, you feel better about yourself, make a great first impression, and interact with others more confidently, all of which helps you build relationships and become a more influential man. Dressing well is also something you do for the benefit of those around you; as Russell Smith, author of *Men's Style*, puts it: "think of your appearance as a gift to others." Not only is a stylish man pleasant to look at, but in dressing appropriately for special events, he adds to the atmosphere and ethos of an occasion—he contributes to everyone having an extraordinary, memorable time, and feeling like they've escaped their everyday lives.

The word "artificial" in fact comes from the Latin *artificialis* which means "of or belonging to art." All art is man-made, and yet it brings beauty and life to both the artist and the viewer. Style is just another kind of art, and just like any other, creating it is a skill the artist must practice. The Sartorialist Badge will help you develop that skill and learn the art of style.

SARTORIALIST BADGE REQUIREMENTS

Complete 10 of the following requirements:

1. Read 2 of the following books:
    a. *Men's Style* by Russell Smith
    b. *Dressing the Man* by Alan Flusser
    c. *Esquire Handbook of Style*
    d. *Dress Like a Man* by Antonio Centeno
2. Get your measurements done by a tailor. Record them for future use.
3. Explain the principles of good fit to a friend.
4. Buy a garment off the rack, or choose a garment that's currently in your closet but is too baggy/loose/big for you, and take it to a tailor to be altered to fit you properly.

5. Build a minimal, but interchangeable wardrobe. This will differ from man to man. If you're a high-powered attorney who has to wear a suit every day, you'll be focusing on shirts and ties. If you work in a more casual environment, you'll incorporate jeans and printed shirts. But the basics are common to every man:

    a. Perform a wardrobe audit. Get rid of all the clothing you haven't worn in a year (excluding formal/special occasion wear).

    b. Then acquire these basics; if you're on a budget, take your time, and acquire pieces as slowly as you need to:

        i. A charcoal or navy suit
        ii. Pair of dark, simple jeans
        iii. Pair of khakis
        iv. A sports jacket
        v. 2-3 solid or small-patterned light-colored dress shirts (white and light blues)
        vi. Lightweight solid-colored sweater
        vii. Pair of black dress shoes and matching belt
        viii. 2 pairs of casual shoes (dress boot, brogue, saddle shoe, chukka boot)
        ix. Casual belt
        x. 2 neckties

    If you've got those basics, you'll be ready for almost any occasion. After that, slowly acquire pieces you simply enjoy wearing.

6. Visit a thrift store and create one sharp-looking outfit from the items you find there. Be sure to get them tailored if they need it!

7. Pick a style icon from film, business, or politics who embodies the kind of style you'd like to develop yourself, spend time thinking about what it is about his style you admire, and then create an outfit inspired by him.

SARTORIALIST BADGE

8. Know how to tie all of the following tie knots, and the best time to use each:
   a. Bowtie
   b. Windsor
   c. Half-Windsor
   d. Four-in-Hand
9. Know how to shine your shoes and shine all your shoes that need it.
10. Demonstrate how to properly iron a dress shirt and a pair of dress pants.
11. Learn how to talk to your barber and communicate with him how you want your hair cut.
12. Establish a morning and evening grooming routine and adhere to it every day for 4 consecutive weeks.
13. Put together what you think is a sharp outfit for one of the following occasions and post a picture in the Gymnasium for feedback:
    a. Work
    b. Night out
    c. Special event (wedding, job interview, party, conference, etc.)

For additional resources, visit stren.life/style.

SARTORIALIST BADGE

SCOUT BADGE

A scout is the eyes and ears of any military unit. Physical endurance, navigation skills, and a keen, observant eye are paramount. He must be comfortable in unfamiliar territory. The Scout Badge will equip you with these skills and attributes in spades. This badge isn't for the faint of heart, but neither is the job of a scout. Upon completion of this badge, you'll have the confidence to navigate any landscape without getting lost.

SCOUT BADGE REQUIREMENTS

Complete all of the following requirements:

1. Fitness Requirements:
    a. Walk a mile in 15 minutes.
    b. Walk 30 miles in 14 hours.
    c. Run 100 yards in 17 seconds.
    d. Run 50 yards in 8 seconds.
    e. Low crawl 50 yards in 2 minutes.

     f. Swim 100 yards in 1:45 seconds (pool) or 2 minutes (open water).
2. Knowing Your Environment:
     a. Find north without a compass in the following circumstances:
          i. During the day
          ii. On a cloudy day
          iii. At night
     b. Determine the time without a watch using the following methods:
          i. Make a sundial using a stick pointing north
          ii. Use hands and horizon method to determine sunset time
     c. Predict the weather each morning for a week using only natural phenomena. Write down your predictions in a notebook.
     d. Estimate the following without using a tape measure:
          i. Height of a tree
          ii. Width of a river
          iii. The distance of a far off object
3. Compass Work
     a. Take a bearing with a compass on any object in the field.
     b. Demonstrate knowledge of magnetic declination in one of the following ways:
          i. Adjust compass for local magnetic declination
          ii. Write down how much you'd have to subtract or add to compass bearing in order to get true bearing
     c. Measure a bearing between 2 points on a map using a compass.
     d. Plot a bearing on a map using the bearing acquired from your compass.

e. Orient map to true north using compass.

f. Acquire the line and area points for 3 points on a map.

g. Demonstrate how to box an obstacle.

4. Tracking Distance Walked

   a. Make Ranger Beads.

   b. Determine pace count for 100 meters.

   c. Use ranger beads to track a 16 km hike.

5. Land Navigate Using Topographic Map and Compass

   a. Produce 5 MGRS 8-digit grid coordinates in a wilderness area that allows for free walking (find the website to use on the resources page).

   b. Plot these 5 points on map using military protractor. Label them 1, 2, 3, 4, 5.

   c. Using military protractor scale, measure distance in kilometers between each plot point.

   d. Using protractor, determine bearings that you'll use in order to arrive at each destination point you plotted on map.

   e. Begin at starting plot and navigate to each of the 5 plot points on map using coordinates, distance, and bearings you've recorded. Use ranger beads to measure distance traveled, use compass to measure bearings.

6. Take 16 km hike and explore and record things seen, condition of roads/trails, types of vegetation and wildlife. From field notes, draw a rough map of the area.

For additional resources, visit stren.life/scout.

SHARP SHOOTER BADGE

Since the invention of gunpowder, firearms have been one of man's trustiest and most powerful tools.

And with that great power, comes great responsibility.

Guns can serve as both satisfying recreation, and potent protection, but only if their owner knows how to handle them safely, correctly, and effectively. Such training can save not only the life of the handler, but the lives of those they want to keep safe.

Earning the Sharp Shooter Badge will put you on the road to becoming a skilled and responsible gun owner. You'll by no means be an expert by the time you complete this badge—that takes years of training and practice. But you'll hopefully gain a basic understanding of how guns work, a healthy respect for firearms, a desire to continue your training, and a love for plinking.

SHARP SHOOTER BADGE REQUIREMENTS

Complete all of the following mandatory requirements:

1. Explain the Four Cardinal Rules of firearms safety to a friend.
2. Take one course or class (minimum 3 hours) taught by a professional that covers either pistol, rifle, or shotgun shooting.

Choose one of the firearms below and complete all of its respective requirements:

Pistol

1. Demonstrate how to properly unload and clear a semi-automatic pistol.
2. Demonstrate how to properly hold, aim, and fire a pistol.
3. Demonstrate how to perform the 4-step pistol draw.
4. Demonstrate how to clear an ammo malfunction.
5. Demonstrate how to re-load a semi-automatic pistol in a stationary position.
6. Perform the 5x5 Handgun Skill Test in 41 seconds or less.

Rifle

1. Demonstrate how to properly unload and clear a semi-automatic, bolt action, or lever rifle.
2. Demonstrate how to properly hold, aim, and fire a rifle.
3. Demonstrate how to clear an ammo malfunction.

4. Demonstrate how to re-load a semi-automatic or other type of rifle in a stationary position.
5. Perform a 5-shot rifle zero group test and explain what the results tell you about your rifle and your shooting mechanics.
6. Perform the 5x5 Carbine Test in 46 seconds or less.

Shotgun

1. Demonstrate how to properly unload and clear a pump or semi-automatic shotgun.
2. Demonstrate how to properly hold, aim, and fire a shotgun.
3. Demonstrate how to clear a malfunction on a pump action or semi-automatic shotgun.
4. Demonstrate how to properly load a pump or semi-automatic shotgun.
5. Do a skeet shoot. Hit at least 10 clay pigeons.

For additional resources, visit stren.life/sharpshooter.

SHARP SHOOTER BADGE

SHAVING BADGE

Shaving. It's something many men do almost every day, and it usually seems like a chore. You slop on your green goo from a can and scrape your face with the latest 6-bladed razor that costs an arm and a leg.

But it doesn't have to be that way. By using the shaving tools and techniques that your grandpa and great-grandpas used, you can save yourself some money, get a better and closer shave, and turn this daily chore into an enjoyable and meditative masculine ritual.

The Shaving Badge will put you on the path to reclaiming and mastering this classic ritual for yourself.

SHAVING BADGE REQUIREMENTS

Complete all of the following mandatory requirements:

1. Lather with a badger brush and shave with a safety razor at least 30 times (non-consecutive).
2. Demonstrate how to properly strop a straight razor.

3. Lather with a badger brush and shave with a straight razor at least 30 times (non-consecutive).

Complete 4 of the following requirements:

1. Shave with cold water for at least 3 times and compare the experience with hot; evaluate which kind of water works better for your face.
2. Make your own shaving cream.
3. Make a hot towel at home for a barbershop shave experience.
4. Buy and restore an antique safety or straight razor.
5. Reward yourself for mastering the art of shaving, by getting someone else to do it for you! Get a straight razor shave from a barber.

For additional resources, visit stren.life/shaving.

SHAVING BADGE

SHEEPDOG BADGE

An old Vietnam veteran once told Lt. Col. Dave Grossman that the world can be divided into three kinds of people: sheep, wolves, and sheepdogs.

Most people are sheep. This isn't pejorative. It simply is meant to convey the fact that most people are kind, gentle, peaceful, and passive. While most people are good-natured, they simply don't know how to deal with evil and dangerous people because for the most part, they don't encounter and interact with evil and dangerous people in their day-to-day lives. Like sheep, they largely move about with those who are like them, doing as others do and going with the flow.

Wolves are the bad guys. They prey on the sheep. They take advantage of the sheep's tendency to be inexperienced with evil, unprepared for attack, and caught flat-footed when a crisis arises.

Then there are the sheepdogs. They're society's guardians. They protect the sheep from the wolves. Human sheepdogs live among the people they protect. They're kind to those who they watch over, but vigilantly watch for danger, and have the capacity to do violence to those who would harm the "flock."

Which one are you?

If you decide to become a sheepdog, a man who refuses to be a victim to wolves and won't let others be victims either, you must accept the responsibility to train yourself mentally, morally, and physically for the responsibility. The Sheepdog Badge will help you begin your journey to becoming an alert, skillful guardian.

SHEEPDOG BADGE REQUIREMENTS

Earn the following prerequisite badges:

1. Fighter Badge
2. Sharp Shooter Badge
3. First Aid Badge

Read these 4 required Art of Manliness series/articles:

1. Are You a Sheep or Sheepdog?
2. How to Develop Situational Awareness
3. How to Treat Your Family Like VIPs
4. What to Do in an Active Shooter Situation

Complete 10 of the following requirements:

1. Read 2 of the following books:
    a. *The Unthinkable: Who Survives When Disaster Strikes—And Why* by Amanda Ripley
    b. *Left of Bang* by Patrick van Horne
    c. *Warrior Mindset* by Dr. Michael Asken, Loren W. Christensen, Dave Grossman and Human Factor Research

    d. *On Combat* by Dave Grossman and Loren W. Christensen
    e. *The Survivors Club: The Secrets and Science that Could Save Your Life* by Ben Sherwood
    f. *The Gift of Fear* by Gavin de Becker
    g. *Facing Violence: Preparing for the Unexpected* by Rory Miller
    h. *How to Survive the Most Critical 5 Seconds of Your Life* by Tim Larkin
2. Memorize the Cooper Color Code.
3. Demonstrate tactical breathing.
4. Explain the legality of using violent force in a self-defense situation.
5. Go to a public place like a coffee shop or restaurant with a friend. Have your friend make a mental note of about 10 things about the environment (the number of workers behind the counter, the clothing and sex of the person sitting next to you, how many entries/exits there are, etc.). When you leave and get into the car to head home, have your friend ask you 10 questions like: "How many workers were behind the counter?" "Was the person sitting next to us a man or a woman?" "What color was his/her shirt?" "How many exits were there?" Get 8 out of 10 right.
6. Play Kim's Game for 2 rounds with a set of 24 different objects each time. Get at least 16 objects correct.
7. Create an EDC that will allow you to be prepared for any situation you find yourself in. Consider the following items:
    a. Cash
    b. Lock pick set
    c. Tactical pen
    d. Pocket knife
    e. Small tactical flashlight
    f. Firearm (if licensed and legal to carry)

8. Escape from zip ties and duct tape.
9. Pick a lock.
10. Role play what you would do to verbally defuse or avoid a potentially violent encounter.
11. Slowly demonstrate 5 of the following movements that would cause the most damage to a lethal attacker:
    a. Eye gouge
    b. Groin attack
    c. Throat strike
    d. Kicking/stomping vulnerable parts of body like joints, head, neck, kidneys
    e. Grabbing and pinching a clavicle
    f. Grabbing the trachea
    g. Small joint manipulation (aka, breaking fingers)
    h. Foot stomping
12. Demonstrate how to disarm a knifeman, and explain when you'd want to try to attempt that and when you wouldn't.
13. Demonstrate how to disarm a gunman from the front and behind, and explain when you'd want to attempt that and when you wouldn't.

For required reading and additional resources, visit stren.life/sheepdog.

SOCIAL DYNAMO BADGE

Man is a social creature. Unless you're a monk or a hermit, you interact with people every single day. And each interaction represents a powerful opportunity—to meet your future spouse, a business contact, or a new friend—or simply a chance for connection and an enjoyable, interesting conversation.

Mastering social skills allows you to enter any room with confidence, chat comfortably with strangers, charm the opposite sex, influence potential clients, and simply have a good time with other people wherever you go. It allows you to navigate the world without anxiety, become more influential, and build a network of close friends, enjoyable acquaintances, and strategic allies.

While charisma and personal magnetism are often thought of as inborn traits, they're actually skills that anyone can develop—introverts and extroverts alike. The Social Dynamo Badge will help you practice the skill of charm and allow you to become cool, comfortable, and charming when you interact with others.

SOCIAL DYNAMO BADGE REQUIREMENTS

Complete 5 of the following requirements:

1. Read "Why Your First Impression Matters" and "How to Use Body Language to Create a Dynamite First Impression." Choose 2 tips from the latter article you'd like to work on. Practice the first tip every day for one week during the first impressions you make. Then practice the second tip every day for one week.
2. Read AoM's 3-part series on being charismatic and make a list of 4 tips you want to start incorporating into your interactions with others. Practice 1 tip every day for 1 week each.
3. Take the "21-Day Small Talk Challenge": You must attempt to talk to at least one stranger each day for 21 days.
4. Attend an event where you don't know any of the other guests/participants. Talk to at least 5 people at the event before you leave.
5. Read our article, "How to Enter a Room Like a Boss." Pick 3 tips from the article you wish to try, and practice them during at least one entrance into a room where others will see you.
6. Read 2 of AoM's conversation articles: "The Art of Conversation: 5 Dos and Don'ts" and "How to Avoid Conversational Narcissism." During subsequent conversations, practice employing their tips—listening attentively, asking questions, introducing interesting topics to talk about, etc.

For required reading and additional resources, visit stren.life/social.

TRACKER BADGE

"*The trailer has the key to a new storehouse of nature's secrets...his fairy godmother has indeed conferred on him a wonderful gift in opening his eyes to the foot-writing of the trail. It is like giving sight to the blind man, like the rolling away of fogs from a mountain view, and the trailer comes closer than others to the heart of the woods.*

Dowered with a precious power is he,
He drinks where others sipped,
And wild things write their lives for him
In endless manuscript."

–Ernest Seton, Manual of the Woodcraft Indians, 1915

> *"I do not hesitate to say that faithful study of the language of footprints in all its details will be certain to develop your insight as well as your powers of observation."*

> —Charles "Ohiyesa" Eastman (Sioux tribesman), *Indian Scout Talks*, 1915

Learning how to track and identify the footprints of both animals and humans is an ancient and largely forgotten art—one that's not only important for hunters, but also enhances any outdoorsman's experience in the wild. It's fascinating to know what creatures are sharing the woods with you, and trying to track them down by following their trail is a lot of fun. Learning how to read tracks allows you to pick up on the little dramas enacted by wildlife that usually go unnoticed by the human eye. It's thus a skill that both deepens your understanding of nature and heightens your all-important powers of observation.

TRACKER BADGE REQUIREMENTS

Complete all of the following requirements:

1. Identify and follow the tracks of 4 different wild animals far enough that you can determine their gait and the direction they were traveling.
2. Make a tracker's aging stand and study/maintain it for at least 6 weeks.
3. Have a friend hide himself in the woods at least a mile out from your location, without your looking; then track him down.
4. Get close enough to 4 wild animals to take a picture of them. Must include:
   a. 1 bird away from its nest

b. 1 bird in its nest
c. 1 animal as big as or smaller than a rabbit
d. 1 animal bigger than a rabbit

For additional resources, visit stren.life/tracker.

VIRTUE BADGE

Benjamin Franklin was the quintessential self-made man. From humble beginnings, he rose to become a successful printer, scientist, musician, and author. In his spare time, he helped found a country.

The key to Franklin's success was his drive to constantly improve himself—mentally, professionally, and morally. His quest for excellence in the latter pursuit began in earnest at age 20. It was then that he conceived of a program that would motivate and push him to adopt more virtuous habits. Ever the moral pragmatist, he drew up a list of 13 virtues, and created a chart on which to keep track of his progress in living them. Each week he would specifically focus on one virtue while also keeping track of the others. He would then move on to the next virtue and so on, eventually going through four cycles of each of the virtues in a single year.

When he failed to live up to the virtues on a particular day, he would place a mark on the chart. When Franklin first started out on his program he found himself putting marks in the book more often than he wanted. But as time went by, he saw the marks diminish.

Though Franklin never attained his goal of "moral perfection," he felt that the effort had still greatly improved his life:

> *"Tho' I never arrived at the perfection I had been so ambitious of obtaining, but fell far short of it, yet I was, by the endeavour, a better and a happier man than I otherwise should have been if I had not attempted it."*

Take Franklin's 13-week virtue challenge yourself, and you'll improve your character, feel happier, and earn your Virtue Badge to boot.

VIRTUE BADGE REQUIREMENTS

Complete all of the following requirements:

1. Read our series on Benjamin Franklin's virtues.
2. Complete one 13-week cycle of Benjamin Franklin's virtue project.

For required reading and additional resources, visit stren.life/virtue.

WILDERNESS
SURVIVAL BADGE

It's every man's worst nightmare and most satisfying fantasy: You're stranded in the wild with nothing but the clothes on your back, a pocketknife, and your wits.

It's a nightmare because, well, you're in the wild and exposed to the elements. Death is often the outcome for modern humans in this situation.

But many men daydream about wilderness survival scenarios because they want to know: "Could I master nature like my ancestors of old? Would I be able to keep my carcass alive or have I become so soft and inept that I would die within a day?"

Even though we simultaneously fear and fantasize about braving the wild like some modern Jeremiah Johnson, most of us would probably want to avoid the situation as much as possible.

But...

There's always the chance fate could force such a disaster upon you. Maybe you're hunting or backpacking and you get lost. Or you crash your small two-seater plane in the middle of the Canadian wilderness *Hatchet*-style.

Should you find yourself in such a situation, the Wilderness Survival Badge will give you the foundational skills and knowledge necessary for staying alive and making it back to civilization.

Even if you never have to use these skills in a survive-or-die situation, they're still incredibly fun and satisfying to learn and practice.

WILDERNESS SURVIVAL BADGE REQUIREMENTS

Earn the following prerequisite badges:

1. Fire Builder Badge
2. Scout Badge
3. First Aid Badge
4. Knotsmanship Badge

Complete 8 of the following requirements:

1. Explain the following to a friend:
   a. The 7 wilderness survival priorities
   b. Tactics to use to avoid panic when lost in the wild
   c. How to survive encounters with bears, mountain lions, and poisonous snakes
2. Build a wilderness survival kit.
3. Demonstrate rescue signals using 3 of the following methods:
   a. Mirror
   b. Whistle
   c. Fire
   d. Rocks
4. Demonstrate how to acquire water in the wild using 2 of following methods:
   a. Collect rain water using a tarp or poncho

     b. Collect morning dew
     c. Collect plant transpiration
     d. Dig an underground still
5. Purify water from a wild source using 2 different methods.
6. Find and identify 5 edible plants in the wild.
7. Build a spring snare or deadfall trap for small game.
8. Build a bottle trap to catch fish.
9. Build a hunting/fishing gig to catch fish in a stream or pond.
10. Build a survival shelter of a design of your choosing; sleep in it for the night.

For additional resources, visit stren.life/survival.

"CITIZENSHIP IN A REPUBLIC"

By Theodore Roosevelt, 1910

It is not the critic who counts; not the man who points out how the strong man stumbles, or where the doer of deeds could have done them better. The credit belongs to the man who is actually in the arena, whose face is marred by dust and sweat and blood; who strives valiantly; who errs, who comes short again and again, because there is no effort without error and shortcoming; but who does actually strive to do the deeds; who knows great enthusiasms, the great devotions; who spends himself in a worthy cause; who at the best knows in the end the triumph of high achievement, and who at the worst, if he fails, at least fails while daring greatly, so that his place shall never be with those cold and timid souls who neither know victory nor defeat.

SOCRATES ON THE IMPORTANCE OF PHYSICAL FITNESS

From the *Memorabilia*, c. 371 BC
By Xenophon

In his Memorabilia, *Xenophon, a student of Socrates, shares a dialogue between Socrates and one of Socrates' disciples named Epigenes. On noticing his companion was in poor condition for a young man, the philosopher admonished him by saying, "You look as if you need exercise, Epigenes." To which the young man replied, "Well, I'm not an athlete, Socrates." Socrates then offered the following response.*

Just as much as the competitors entered for Olympia. Or do you count the life and death struggle with their enemies, upon which, it may be, the Athenians will enter, but a small thing? Why, many, thanks to their bad condition, lose their life in the perils of war or save it disgracefully: many, just for this same cause, are taken prisoners, and then either pass the rest of their days, perhaps, in slavery of the hardest kind, or, after meeting with cruel sufferings and paying, sometimes, more than they have, live on, destitute and in misery. Many, again, by their bodily weakness earn infamy, being thought cowards. Or do you despise these, the rewards of bad condition, and think that you can easily endure such things? And yet I suppose that what has to be borne by anyone who takes care to keep his body in good condition is far lighter and far pleasanter than these things. Or is it that you think bad condition healthier and generally more serviceable than good, or do you despise the effects of good condition? And yet the results of physical fitness are the direct opposite of those

---

that follow from unfitness. The fit are healthy and strong; and many, as a consequence, save themselves decorously on the battle-field and escape all the dangers of war; many help friends and do good to their country and for this cause earn gratitude; get great glory and gain very high honors, and for this cause live henceforth a pleasanter and better life, and leave to their children better means of winning a livelihood.

I tell you, because military training is not publicly recognized by the state, you must not make that an excuse for being a whit less careful in attending to it yourself. For you may rest assured that there is no kind of struggle, apart from war, and no undertaking in which you will be worse off by keeping your body in better fettle. For in everything that men do the body is useful; and in all uses of the body it is of great importance to be in as high a state of physical efficiency as possible. Why, even in the process of thinking, in which the use of the body seems to be reduced to a minimum, it is matter of common knowledge that grave mistakes may often be traced to bad health. And because the body is in a bad condition, loss of memory, depression, discontent, insanity often assail the mind so violently as to drive whatever knowledge it contains clean out of it. But a sound and healthy body is a strong protection to a man, and at least there is no danger then of such a calamity happening to him through physical weakness: on the contrary, it is likely that his sound condition will serve to produce effects the opposite of those that arise from bad condition. And surely a man of sense would submit to anything to obtain the effects that are the opposite of those mentioned in my list.

Besides, it is a disgrace to grow old through sheer carelessness before seeing what manner of man you may become by developing your bodily strength and beauty to their highest limit. But you cannot see that, if you are careless; for it will not come of its own accord.

"THE VALUE OF DOING"

From *The Woodcraft Manual for Boys,* 1923
By *Ernest Thompson Seton*

Our grandfathers alone in the wilderness, were sufficient unto themselves, for they were true Woodcrafters—they mastered the things about them. Conditions have changed, and now most of these things have been taken from the home to the factory, so the old home training is no longer in reach.

The big value of all this knowledge was in that it bestowed power. For learning to do gives more power to do, and when you let someone else do a thing for you, you eventually lose the power to do that thing. Through the ability to do have peoples prospered and nations become great.

When the Romans put in the hands of slaves the doing of everything, they thereby lost the power to do, and were defeated by themselves in their national life and then by their enemies in battle. The Vikings sailed their ships fearlessly and far, for they had proved themselves on many seas. In time of stress, each leader took the helm of his own ship; and the proud boast often heard among these world-subduing northern folk was: "I am a noble. My father owns his own forge." Always in the world's history, those who valued the ability to do have been strong and sturdy. The Persians' battle flag in their strongest time was a blacksmith's apron. Emerson recognized the value of doing things well when he said: "If a man can write a better book, preach a better sermon, or make a better mousetrap than his neighbor, though he live in the woods, the world will make a beaten path to his doorway."

So the Woodcraft Boy of today will learn to do, if he would be happy and healthful; for life is made worthwhile, not by the few great moments, but the making of the daily life pleasant and full of meaning. The difference in lives is largely in what one knows and can do. One is of value in the office from this standpoint.

Probably nothing is sadder than to go into a home where everything is bought ready prepared; clothing ready made, food bought in small quantities at a delicatessen shop, amusement had at the movies or at some place where it can be bought. The clothing is commonplace—no brain or pride has gone into the making; the food was bought in a hurry and haphazardly. The amusements are often flat, and mostly superficial.

Oh, Woodcraft Boy, would you really live? Then begin, not by dreaming of some new field to enter or new worlds to conquer, but by knowing and using all the things about you. Know the pleasure of workmanship, the joy that comes from things made well by your own hands, the happiness which comes from closer touch with the fundamental things of life and the consciousness of being of value to the world.

"THE GREATEST SPORTING PROPOSITION"

From *It's a Good Old World*, 1920
By Bruce Barton

Sir Walter Raleigh was one of the ablest and most attractive men of his time. Yet he made this fundamental mistake: he picked out the wrong thing to live for.

Looking about to see what was most worthwhile in life, he decided for fame and fortune and thought they might most surely be secured through the favor of Queen Elizabeth. For her favor he demeaned himself, and neglected his wife, and was constantly in petty intrigues unbecoming his talents.

At the end the fickle queen turned upon him and cast him into London Tower. And her successor sent him to the block.

Every age has its quota of Sir Walters: strong men who trade their lives for this or that, and at the close have traded themselves empty-handed.

And no man has more important business than to determine very early what is really worth having—being sure that the object he selects is one that can be depended upon to satisfy him not merely through his full-blooded years, but up through the testing hours at the last.

What is such an object? Money?

I wish that every young man in the world could see, as I once saw, a man who had bartered his soul for money, and who woke one morning to discover that it had vanished overnight. Surely a possession that can so quickly fly away, and that leaves such shriveled souls behind it, cannot be the supreme good.

Fame? Political preferment? Horace Greeley was as famous as any man of his period; he let his ambition carry him into the race for the Presidency, and losing the race, died of a broken heart.

There is a finer formula than either of these. Plato stated it, centuries ago:

> *I therefore, Callicles, am persuaded by these accounts, and consider how I may exhibit my soul before the judge in a healthy condition. Wherefore, disregarding the honors that most men value, and look-*

ing to the truth, I shall endeavor to live as virtuously as I can; and when I die, to die so. And I invite all other men, to the utmost of my power; and you too I in turn invite to this contest, which I affirm surpasses all contests here.

A great game in which the player is a man's best self on the one side, and on the other all the temptations and the disappointments and the buffeting of circumstance.

The game of making yourself the best you can be, let Fate say what it will; of so investing the years and the talents you have as to cause the largest number of people to be glad, the fewest to be sorry, and coming to the end with the least regret.

"Be diligent," wrote Polycarp to Ignatius. "Be diligent. Be sober as God's athlete. *Stand like a beaten anvil.*"

I do not know how any man can stand like a beaten anvil who has only money to stand upon; or only a reputation that may vanish as quickly as it came; or a ribbon which is pinned on his coat to-day and may be taken off to-morrow.

But let him have invested his life in the mastery and the cultivation of his own best self, and he has laid up riches that cannot be lost.

Whatever obstacles, whatever disappointments may come, are merely added chances against him, contributing to the zest of the contest.

And in the end he has this surpassing reward, a clear conscience and a vision unafraid—the prize of the victor in the greatest sporting proposition in the world.

THE CHOICE OF HERCULES

From the *Memorabilia*, c. 371 B.C.
By Xenophon

---

*Xenophon (430–354 B.C.) was an ancient Greek historian
and student of the philosopher Socrates. His* Memorabilia
*is a collection of Socratic dialogues which purports to
record the defense Socrates made for himself during his
trial before the Athenians. While arguing against indolence
and for the beneficial effects of labor, Socrates cites a story
told by the Sophist Prodicus: The Choice of Hercules.*

When Hercules was in that part of his youth in which
it was natural for him to consider what course of life he
ought to pursue, he one day retired into a desert, where
the silence and solitude of the place very much favored
his meditations.

As he was musing on his present condition, and very
much perplexed in himself, on the state of life he should
choose, he saw two women of a larger stature than ordinary, approaching towards him. One of them had a very
noble air, and graceful deportment; her beauty was natural and easy, her person clean and unspotted, her motions
and behavior full of modesty, and her raiment was white
as snow. The other wanted all the native beauty and pro-
portion of the former; her person was swelled, by luxu-
ry and ease, to a size quite disproportioned and uncome-
ly. She had painted her complexion, that it might seem
fairer and more ruddy than it really was, and endeavored
to appear more graceful than ordinary in her bearing, by
a mixture of affectation in all her gestures. She cast her
eyes frequently upon herself, then turned them on those
that were present, to see whether any one regarded her,

---

and now and then looked on the figure she made in her own shadow.

As they drew nearer, the former continued the same composed pace, while the latter, striving to get before her, ran up to Hercules, and addressed herself to him:

"My dear Hercules," says she, "I find you are very much divided in your thoughts, upon the way of life that you ought to choose; be my friend, and follow me; I will lead you into the possession of pleasure, and out of the reach of pain, and remove you from all the noise and disquietude of business. The affairs of either peace or war, shall have no power to disturb you. Your whole employment shall be to make your life easy, and to entertain every sense with its proper gratifications. Sumptuous tables, beds of roses, clouds of perfumes, concerts of music, crowds of beauties, are all in readiness to receive you. Come along with me into this region of delights, this world of pleasure, and bid farewell forever, to care, to pain, to business."

Hercules, hearing the lady talk after this manner, desired to know her name; to which she answered, "My friends, and those who are well acquainted with me, call me Happiness; but my enemies, and those who would injure my reputation, have given me the name of Pleasure."

By this time the other lady came up, who addressed herself to the young hero in a very different manner.

"Hercules," says she, "I offer myself to you, because I know you are descended from the gods, and give proofs of that descent by your love to virtue, and application to the studies proper for your age. This makes me hope you will gain, both for yourself and me, an immortal reputation. But, before I invite you into my society and friendship, I will be open and sincere with you, and must lay down this, as an established truth, that there is nothing truly valuable which can be purchased without pains and labor. The gods have set a price upon every real and noble pleasure. If you would gain the favor of the Deity, you must be at the pains of worshiping him: if the friendship of good men, you must study to oblige them: if you would be honored by your country, you must take care to serve it. In short, if you would be eminent in war or peace, you must become master of all the qualifications that can make you so. These are the only terms and conditions upon which I can propose happiness."

The goddess of Pleasure here broke in upon her discourse: "You see," said she, "Hercules, by her own confession, the way to her pleasures is long and difficult; whereas, that which I propose is short and easy." "Alas!" said the other lady, whose visage glowed with passion, made up of scorn and pity, "what are the pleasures you propose? To eat before you are hungry, drink before you are athirst, sleep before you are tired; to gratify your appetites before they are raised. You never heard the most delicious music, which is the praise of one's own self; nor saw the most beautiful object, which is the work of one's own hands. Your votaries pass away their youth in a dream of mistaken pleasures, while they are hoarding up anguish, torment, and remorse, for old age."

"As for me, I am the friend of gods and of good men, an agreeable companion to the artisan, a household guardian to the fathers of families, a patron and protector of servants, an associate in all true and generous friendships. The banquets of my votaries are never costly, but always delicious; for none eat and drink at them, who are not invited by hunger and thirst. Their slumbers are sound, and their wakings cheerful. My young men have the pleasure of hearing themselves praised by those who are in years; and those who are in years, of being honored by those who are young. In a word, my followers are favored by the gods, beloved by their acquaintance, esteemed by their country, and after the close of their labors, honored by posterity."

"THE CALL"

By Earl H. Emmons

> *Did you ever have a longin' to get out and buck*
> *the trail,*
> *And to face the crashin' lightnin' and the thunder*
> *and the gale?*
> *Not for no partic'lar reason but to give the world*
> *the laugh,*
> *And to show the roarin' elyments you still can stand*
> *the gaff.*
>
> *Don't you ever feel a yearnin' just to try your*
> *luck again*
> *Down the rippin' plungin' rapids with a bunch of*
> *reg'lar men?*
> *Don't you ever sorta hanker for a rough and*
> *risky trip,*
> *Just to prove you're still a livin' and you haven't lost*
> *your grip?*
>
> *Can't you hear the woods a-callin' for to have anoth-*
> *er try*
> *Sleepin' out beneath the spruces with a roof of*
> *moonlit sky,*
> *With the wind a sorta singin' through the branch-*
> *es overhead*
> *And your fire a gaily crackin' and your pipe a-*
> *glowin' red?*
>
> *Don't you often get to feelin' sorta cramped and use-*
> *less there,*
> *Makin' figgers and a-shinin' your pants upon*
> *a chair?*

Don't you yearn to get acquainted once again with
Life and God?
If you don't, then Heaven help you, for you're a dyin'
in yer pod.

"THE JOY OF DOING"

From *Undiscovered Country*, 1946
By Raymond John Baughan

The secret of happiness is in knowing this: that we live by the law of expenditure. We find greatest joy, not in getting, but in expressing what we are. There are tides in the ocean of life, and what comes in depends on what goes out. The currents flow inward only where there is an outlet. Nature does not give to those who will not spend; her gifts are loaned to those who will use them. Empty your lungs and breathe. Run, climb, work, and laugh; the more you give out, the more you shall receive. Be exhausted, and you shall be fed. Men do not really live for honors or for pay; their gladness is not in the taking and holding, but in the doing, the striving, the building, the living. It is a higher joy to teach than to be taught. It is good to get justice, but better to do it; fun to have things, but more to make them. The happy man is he who lives the life of love, not for the honors it may bring, but for the life itself.

NOTES

NOTES

NOTES

NOTES

NOTES

NOTES